CHILTERN WALKS

BUCKINGHAMSHIRE

Nick Moon

This book is one of a series of three which provide a comprehensive coverage of walks throughout the whole of the Chiltern area (as defined by the Chiltern Society). The walks included vary in length from 2.4 to 10.8 miles, but are mainly in the 5- to 7-mile range popular for half-day walks, although suggestions of possible combinations of walks are given for those preferring a full day's walk.

Each walk text gives details of nearby places of interest and is accompanied by a specially drawn map of the route which also indicates local pubs and a skeleton road network.

The author, Nick Moon, has lived in or regularly visited the Chilterns all his life and has, for over 40 years, been an active member of the Chiltern Society's Rights of Way Group, which seeks to protect and improve the area's footpath and bridleway network. Thanks to the help and encouragement of the late Don Gresswell MBE, he was introduced to the writing of books of walks and has since written or contributed to a number of publications in this field.

OTHER PUBLICATIONS BY NICK MOON

Chiltern Walks Trilogy
Chiltern Walks 1:   Hertfordshire, Bedfordshire and
North Buckinghamshire:
Book Castle (new edition) 2007
Chiltern Walks 2:   Buckinghamshire:
Chiltern Society (new edition) 2017
Chiltern Walks 3:   Oxfordshire and West Buckinghamshire:
Book Castle (new edition) 2001

Family Walks
Family Walks 1:   Chilterns - South : Book Castle 1997
Family Walks 2:   Chilterns - North : Book Castle 1998

Oxfordshire Walks
Oxfordshire Walks 1: Oxford, The Cotswolds and The Cherwell
Valley: Book Castle (new edition) 1998
Oxfordshire Walks 2: Oxford, The Downs and The Thames Valley:
Book Castle (new edition) 2002

The d'Arcy Dalton Way across the Oxfordshire Cotswolds and
Thames Valley : CPRE Oxfordshire
(new edition) 2016

The Chiltern Way & Chiltern Way Extensions
Chiltern Society (colour edition) 2017

Circular Walks along the Chiltern Way
Volume 1:   Buckinghamshire and Oxfordshire:
Book Castle (new edition) 2010
Volume 2:   Hertfordshire and Bedfordshire:
Chiltern Society (new edition) 2014

First published May 1991   Revised 1993, 1995, 1997, 2005, 2010

New edition July 2017
by Chiltern Society.

© Nick Moon   Printed by Turville Printing Services

ISBN 978-0-904148-36-7

Contents

CHILTERN WALKS: BUCKINGHAMSHIRE:-

POSSIBLE LONGER WALKS PRODUCED BY
COMBINING WALKS DESCRIBED IN THE BOOK

Walks			Miles	Km
1	+ 16		12.7	20.5
1	+ 16	+ 17	18.8	30.2
			or	
			18.4	29.6
4	+ 5		11.9	19.2
4	+ 5	+ 6	20.5	33.1
5	+ 6		15.9	25.7
9	+ 11		18.6	30.0
10	+ 11		16.4	26.4
			or	
			16.6	26.8
13	+ 15		11.1	17.8
13	+ 19		9.9	15.9
13	+ 19	+ 15	15.3	24.7
16	+ 17		12.2	19.7
20	+ 28A		16.5	26.6
20	+ 28B		14.2	22.9
21	+ 25		12.0	19.4
25	+ 26		18.3	29.5
26	+ 29		16.1	25.9
26	+ 29	+ 27	22.8	36.7
			or	
			22.1	35.6
27	+ 29		14.1	22.7
			or	
			13.4	21.6

Cover photograph : Looking back towards The Hale (Walk 5).

© Nick Moon

Introduction

This book of walks is one of three covering the whole of the Chilterns from the Goring Gap on the River Thames to the Hitchin Gap in North Hertfordshire. As the Buckinghamshire Chilterns account for well over a third of the Chiltern area, it has proved necessary to omit certain parts of them from this volume, as only in this way could a reasonably equitable spread of the walks across the Chilterns be achieved. The area to the west of a line from Princes Risborough to Marlow is included in the volume covering the Oxfordshire and West Buckinghamshire Chilterns, while the detached area around Ivinghoe forms part of the Hertfordshire, Bedfordshire and North Buckinghamshire volume. Nevertheless the area which remains, extending from the escarpment between Princes Risborough and Tring in the northwest to the Thames and Colne valleys in the south and east, is one of considerable variety, with a whole series of inviting landscapes to explore.

On the northwestern edge, there is the escarpment, parts of which are very steep, where woodland is interspersed with spectacular downland. Progressing southeastwards, to the east of the Wendover Gap, there is probably the remotest part of the Buckinghamshire Chilterns in the form of the typical Chiltern ridge and bottom country around The Lee and Cholesbury, while to the south of this gap is the Hampden Country, where one again finds the characteristic Chiltern ridges and bottoms but in a more wooded setting. To the east of Chesham is an upland plateau more typical of Hertfordshire, but bounded by deep valleys which add variety to its walks, while, to the south of Amersham, the wooded hills of the Penn Country offer a surprising sense of remoteness when one considers that they are a mere 25 miles from Central London. On the eastern boundary, the ridge separating the Misbourne and Colne valleys also offers some quiet rural areas with extensive views to the east and south and even the Colne valley with its flooded gravel pits and the Grand Union Canal has much to offer for those interested in boats or water fowl. To the south of the A40 and M40, the wide section of the Thames valley between Marlow and Cookham also has much to offer the walker with its picturesque riverside, extensive views from the surrounding hills and attractive areas of woodland on its slopes, while the heavily-wooded plateau to the east around Burnham Beeches and Stoke Poges, interspersed with pleasant shallow bottoms, thanks to the visual and sound-proofing protection of its beautiful woods, also provides plenty of scope for agreeable walks despite its proximity to Slough and the metropolis.

The majority of walks included in this book are in the 5 - 7 mile range, which is justifiably popular for half-day walks, but, for the less energetic or for short winter afternoons, a few shorter versions are indicated in the text, while others can be devised with the assistance of a map. In addition, a number of walks in the 7 - 10 mile range are included for those preferring a leisurely day's walk or for longer spring and summer afternoons, while a list of possible combinations of walks is provided for those favouring a full day's walk of between 10 and 23 miles.

Details of how to reach the starting points by car and where to park are given in the introductory information to each walk and convenient railway stations are shown on the accompanying plan. For up-to-date information on bus services consult the Traveline website at <www.traveline.org.uk> or phone their hotline on 0871-200 22 33.

All the walks described here follow public rights of way, use permissive paths across land owned by public bodies or cross public open space. As the majority of walks cross land used for economic purposes such as agriculture, forestry or the rearing of game, walkers are urged to follow the Country Code at all times:-

- Be **safe** - plan ahead and follow any signs.
- **Leave** gates and property as you find them.
- **Protect** plants and animals, and take your litter home.
- Keep dogs under close **control**.
- **Consider** other people.

Observing these rules helps prevent financial loss to landowners and damage to the environment, as well as the all-too-frequent and sometimes justified bad feeling towards walkers in the countryside.

While it is hoped that the special maps provided with each walk will assist the user to complete the walks without going astray and skeleton details of the surrounding road network are given to enable walkers to shorten the routes in emergency, it is always advisable to take an Ordnance Survey or Chiltern Society map with you to enable you to shorten or otherwise vary the routes without using roads or get your bearings if you do become seriously lost. Details of the appropriate maps are given in the introductory information of each walk.

As for other equipment, readers are advised that where mud warnings are given, the walks are those on which mud remains in dry weather. At other times, all walks are subject to some mud. In any event, proper walking boots are to be recommended at all times as, even when there are no mud problems, hard ruts or rough surfaces make the protection given by boots to the ankles desirable. In addition, the nature of the countryside makes many Chiltern paths prone to overgrowth, particularly in summer. To avoid resultant discomfort, protective clothing is advisable, especially where specific warnings are given.

Some of the walks may be familiar to readers as they were previously published in the ´Walks for Motorists` Chilterns volumes which are now out of print, but about half are completely new or have been radically altered, while all of the old walks have been rechecked and brought up to date. In addition, as the walks are now appearing in the Chiltern Society's name, all the numbers of paths used have been shown on the plans and incorporated into the texts. These numbers, which are also shown on the Society's Footpath Maps, consist of the official County Council footpath number with prefix letters used by the Society to indicate the parish concerned. It is therefore most helpful to use these when reporting any path problems you may find, together, if possible, with the national grid reference for the precise location of the trouble spot, as, in this way, the problem can be identified on the ground with a minimum of time loss in looking for it. National grid references can, however, only be calculated with the help of Ordnance Survey Landranger or Explorer maps and an explanation of how this is done can be found in their keys.

The length of time required for any particular walk depends on a number of factors such as your personal walking speed, the number of hills, stiles etc. to be negotiated, whether or not you stop to rest, eat or drink, investigate places of interest etc. and the number of impediments such as mud, crops, overgrowth, ploughing etc. which you encounter, but generally an average speed of between two and two and a half miles per hour is about right in the Chilterns. It is, however, always advisable to allow extra time if you are limited by the daylight or catching a particular bus or train home in order to avoid your walk developing into a race against the clock.

Should you have problems with any of the paths used on the walks or find that the description given is no longer correct, the author would be most grateful if you could let him have details (c/o The Chiltern Society), so that attempts can be made to rectify the problem or the text can be corrected at the next reprint. Nevertheless, the author hopes that you will not encounter any serious problems and have pleasure from following the walks.

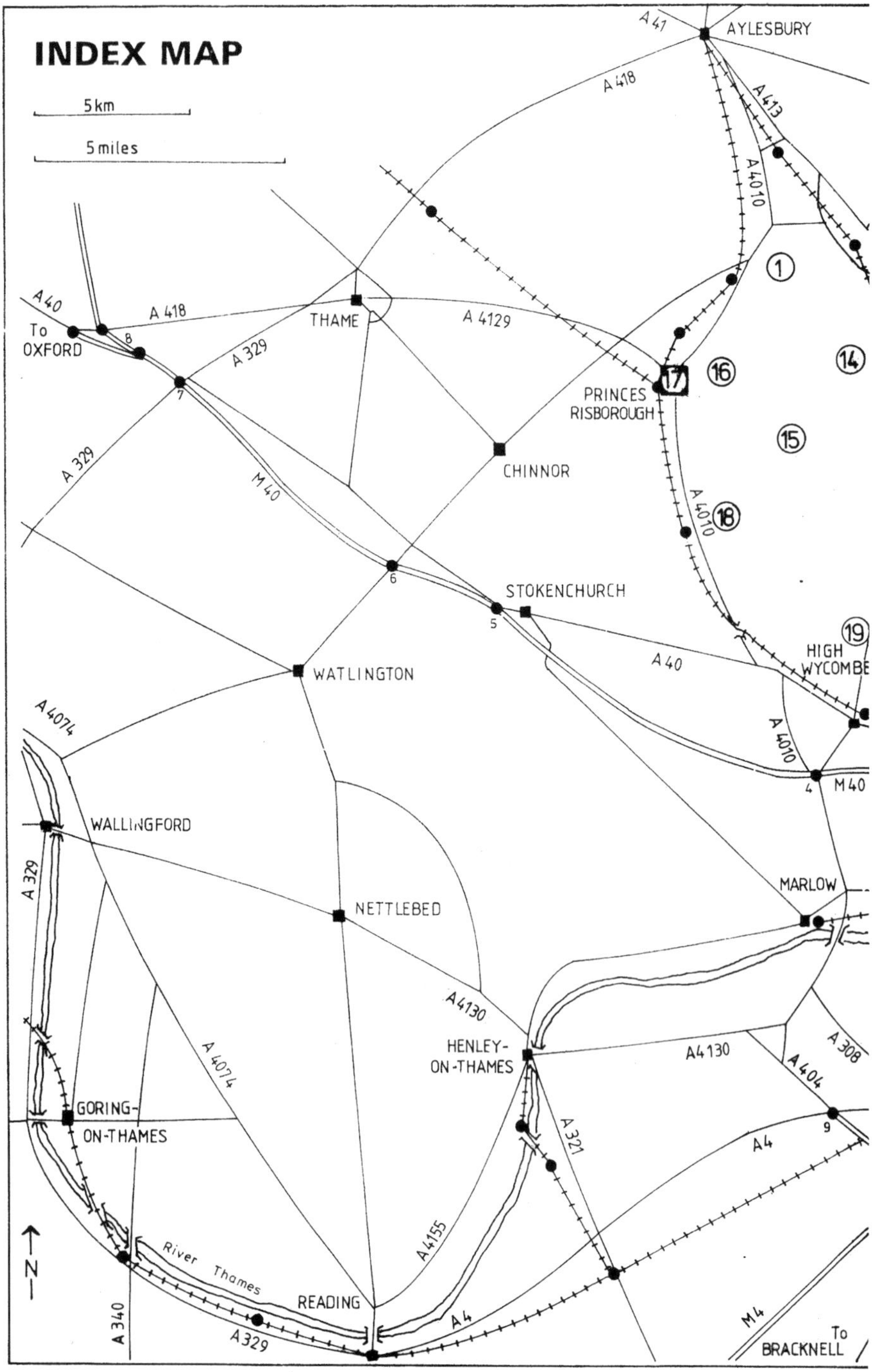

INDEX MAP

5 km

5 miles

AYLESBURY

A 41

A 418

A 413

A 4010

①

A 40

To OXFORD

A 418

A 329

8

7

THAME

A 4129

A 329

M 40

CHINNOR

PRINCES RISBOROUGH

17 ⑯ ⑭

⑮

A 4010 ⑱

19

HIGH WYCOMBE

6

STOKENCHURCH

5

A 40

A 4010

4 M 40

WATLINGTON

A 4074

WALLINGFORD

A 329

NETTLEBED

MARLOW

A 4130

A 4074

GORING-ON-THAMES

HENLEY-ON-THAMES

A 4130

A 308

A 404

A 321

A 4

9

N

A 340

River Thames

A 4155

READING

A 329

A 4

M 4

To BRACKNELL

8

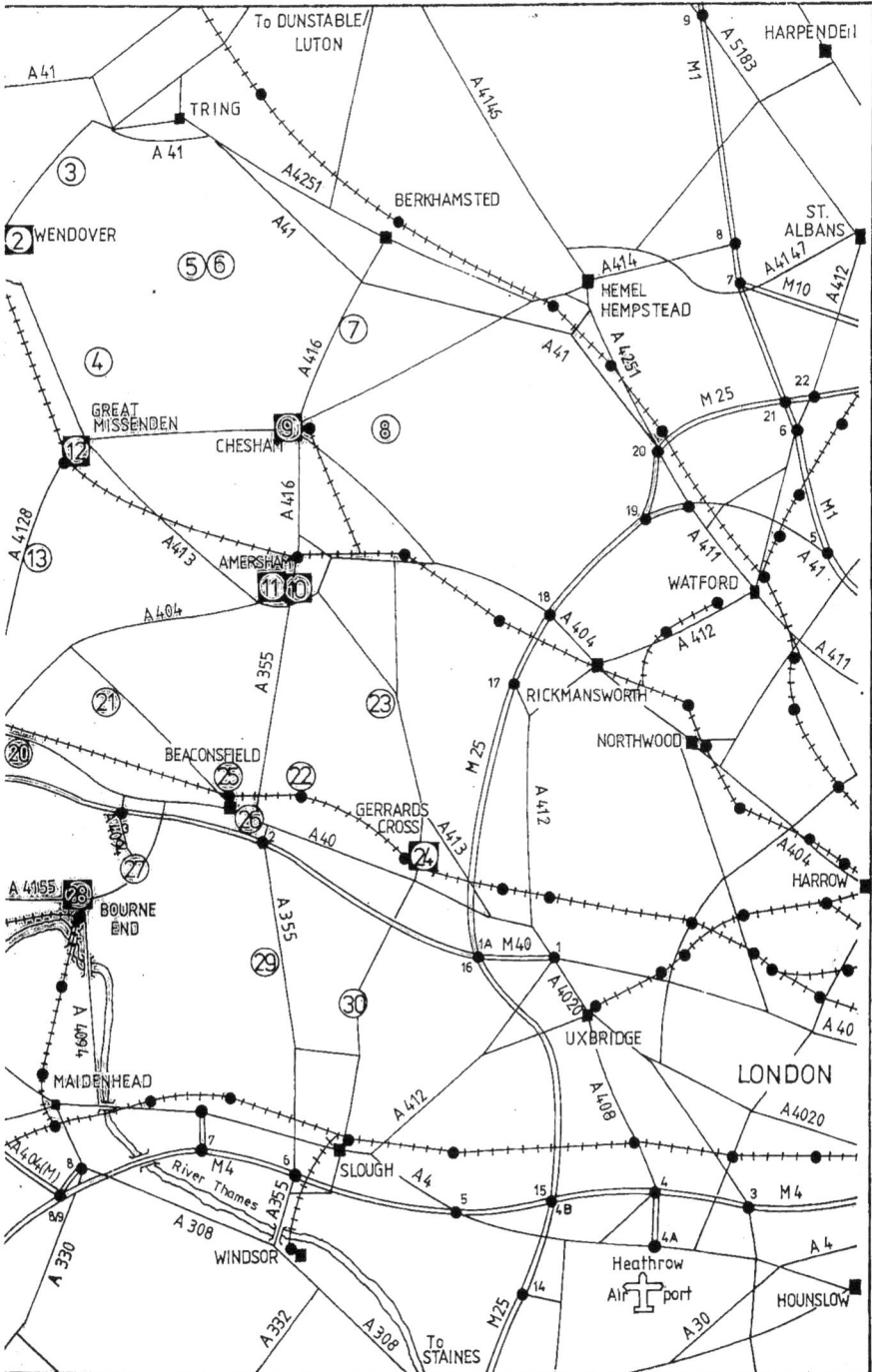

Chiltern
Society

We care for the Chilterns

The Chiltern Society

The Chiltern Society aims to conserve and protect the natural beauty, environment and heritage of the Chilterns. The Society's Rights of Way Group actively protects and restores open access land and public rights of way in the Chilterns — some 5,000 paths. It has surveyed every individual path and takes up irregularities with parish, district or county councils to preserve and enhance public rights. The charity has over 7,000 members and organises weekly walks and cycle rides, as well as volunteer work parties to carry out footpath maintenance and other conservation projects.

We welcome new members - come and join people like you who love the Chilterns. For more details please contact:

The Chiltern Society,
The White Hill Centre,
White Hill,
Chesham,
Buckinghamshire HP5 1AG.

Tel. : 01494-771250.
Email : office@chilternsociety.org.uk
Website : www.chilternsociety.org.uk

WALK 1   Ellesborough (Butler's Cross)

Length of Walk: 6.2 miles / 10.0 Km
Starting Point: Crossroads by the 'Russell Arms' and
Ellesborough Village Hall at Butler's Cross.
Grid Ref: SP843070
Maps: OS Landranger Sheet 165
OS Explorer Sheet 181 (or old Sheet 2)
Chiltern Society FP Map No.3
How to get there / Parking: Butler's Cross, 1.7 miles west of
Wendover, may be reached from the town by following the
Princes Risborough road for 1.7 miles to a crossroads by the
'Russell Arms' at Butler's Cross. Here turn right into
Chalkshire Road and look for a suitable place to park.

Ellesborough, at the foot of the Chiltern escarpment, consists of a series of hamlets connected by ribbons of development, one of which is Butler's Cross where the village pub, shop and post office and the village hall are situated. Despite its small population, the parish is of national significance as it contains Chequers, the country retreat of prime ministers and the imposing fifteenth-century parish church on its prominent hillock at the foot of Beacon Hill is regularly attended by prime ministers and has also played host to foreign statesmen.

The walk explores this parish which can boast some of the most spectacular scenery in the Chilterns, soon climbing to the summit of Coombe Hill with its panoramic views of the surrounding hills and the Vale of Aylesbury before continuing through characteristic Chiltern woodland to the ridgetop village of Dunsmore. It then proceeds through more woodland to enter Chequers Park at Buckmoorend. Having passed the house at a distance, you circle the slopes of Beacon Hill with more fine views, before returning via Ellesborough church to Butler's Cross.

Starting from the crossroads by the 'Russell Arms' and Ellesborough Village Hall, take Chalkshire Road. After some 350 yards, shortly before a right-hand bend, turn right over a stile by a gate and follow a farm track (path E26) across a field, then between a hedge and a fence to a gate. Here fork left leaving the track and following a right-hand fence straight on to a stile at the far end of the field. Cross this and turn right onto path E22b following a right-hand fence uphill to a stile onto

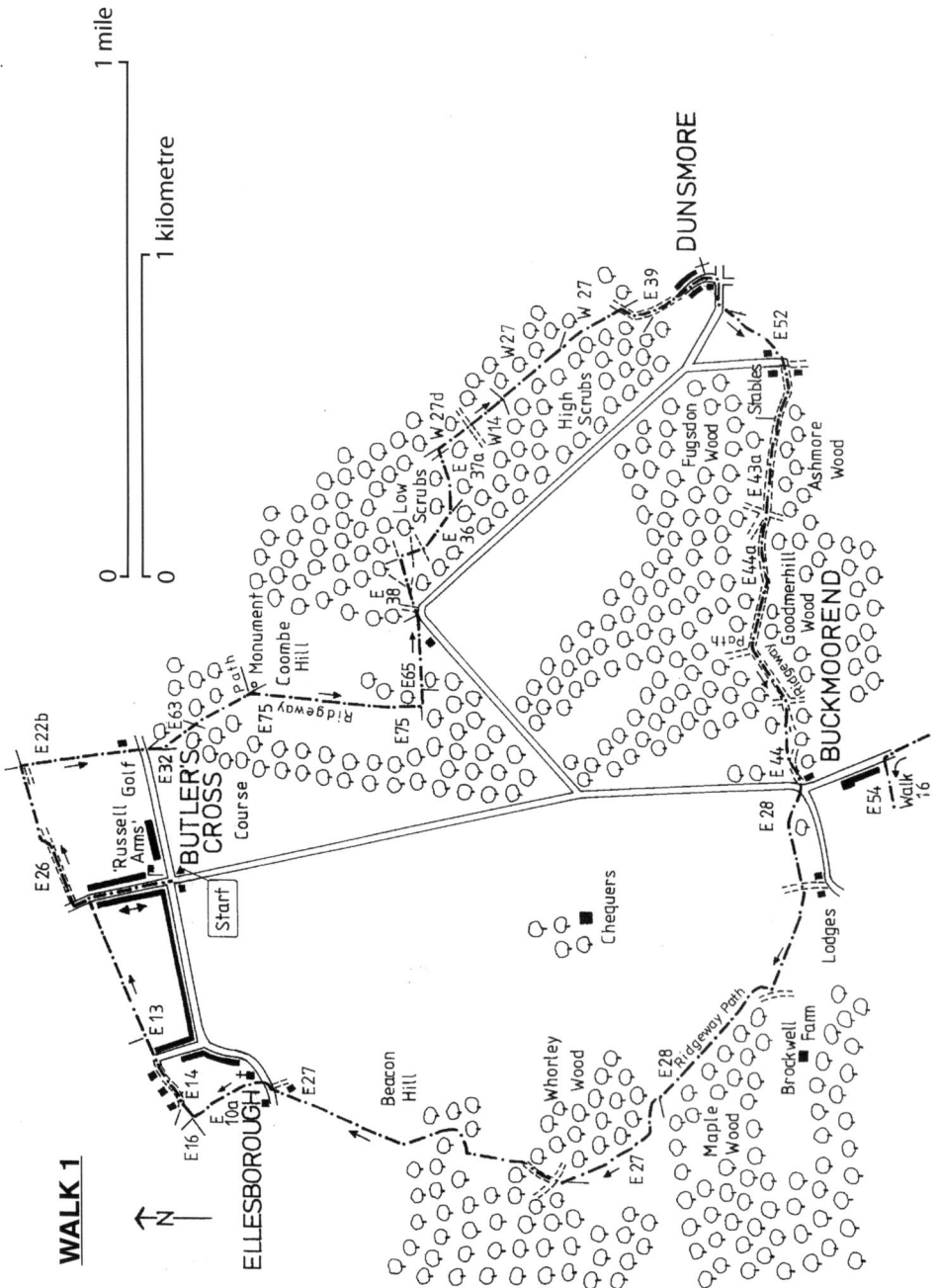

WALK 1

⟵N

ELLESBOROUGH

BUTLER'S CROSS

DUNSMORE

BUCKMOOREND

1 mile

1 kilometre

0

Start

'Russell Arms'

Russell Golf Course

Coombe Hill

Monument

Ridgeway Path

Low Scrubs

High Scrubs

Fugsdon Wood

Stables

Ashmore Wood

Goodmerhill Wood

Ridgeway Path

Chequers

Beacon Hill

Whorley Wood

Maple Wood

Brockwell Farm

Lodges

Walk 16

Ridgeway Path

E 22b

E 26

E63

E32

E13

E16

E14

E10a

E27

E65

E75

E75

E 38

E 36

E 37a

W14

W27

W 27d

W 27

E 39

E 52

E 43a

E 44a

E 44

E 28

E 54

E 27

E 28

Ellesborough Golf Course. Having crossed this, follow a right-hand hedge straight on. Where the hedge turns right, leave it and continue straight on through a group of trees and between two areas of dense scrub. Now pass just right of the clubhouse to a hedge gap onto the Wendover road.

Cross this busy road carefully and take the right-hand of two bridleways (E32) straight on through gates on the edge of woodland, then immediately fork left onto path E63, climbing through a squeeze-stile into the woodland. The path becomes progressively steeper and, on leaving the woodland, becomes steeper still before reaching the monument at the summit of Coombe Hill erected in 1904 in memory of soldiers killed in the Boer War.

After stopping to admire the superb panoramic views from this point 852 feet above sea level, pass right of the monument and take the Ridgeway (path E75) keeping right of the bushes ahead and continuing just below the ridgetop for over a third of a mile until you reach a fenceline. Here turn left onto path E65 following the fenceline uphill and ignoring a kissing-gate in it where the Ridgeway turns off. Where the ground levels out, continue to follow the fenceline, which is concealed by bushes in places, until you reach gates into a car park at a bend in the Dunsmore road.

Here go through a small gate, bear half left across the car park and take signposted path E38 into a coppiced beechwood known as Low Scrubs. Now follow a winding waymarked path, keeping left at a fork and soon reaching a waymarked crossing path. Turn right onto this path (E36) and follow it for nearly 300 yards ignoring all crossing and branching paths. On reaching a second large brackeny clearing, turn left at a waymarked junction onto path E37a into woodland and follow this well-defined path until you reach an old iron fence. Here turn right and take path W27d (later bridleways W14 and W27) alongside this fence for half a mile, disregarding various junctions and later with fences on both sides. On reaching a T-junction of bridleways, fork right onto bridleway E39 and follow it into Dunsmore.

On reaching the end of a village street, keep straight on along it for some 200 yards to a crossroads. Here turn right onto the major road. After about 90 yards turn left over a stile by a gate onto path E52. Bear half right downhill to a stile in the bottom corner of the field. Having crossed this, continue straight on downhill, crossing two further stiles and reaching the end of a road by stables in the valley bottom. Cross the end of this road and take a stony track (bridleway E43a) straight on, soon entering Ashmore Wood. After one third of a mile, at a four-way fork, take path E44a straight on up the valley bottom, soon climbing to cross a ridge. Here the path turns somewhat to the left and you disregard a branching path to the right and continue downhill (now on the Ridgeway again) to a waymarked crossways near the edge of the wood. Now take bridleway E44 straight on into a finger of woodland, soon forking right through a squeeze-stile onto a segregated footpath. After rejoining the bridleway, keep straight on to reach a road junction at Buckmoorend.

Cross the major road and go through a kissing-gate opposite onto path E28 into Chequers Park, then bear slightly left across the park to an electricity pole. Here bear half left to kissing-gates flanking the main drive. Go through these and a further kissing-gate then bear half right to a corner of Maple Wood. Here turn right following a fenced path along the outside edge of the wood to an old gate, where there is a good, but distant view of Chequers itself. Built on the site of an older house by Sir William Hawtrey in 1565, Chequers Court (as it used to be known) was presented to the nation by Lord Lee of Fareham in 1917 for the purpose of providing a country retreat for prime ministers and has served this purpose ever since.

Now continue to follow the outside edge of Maple Wood to reach a kissing-gate near a corner of the park. Go through this and fork right through some bushes to join the outside edge of Whorley Wood, then follow it for a quarter of a mile (leaving the Ridgeway and now on path E27) to reach a gate and kissing-gate into the wood. In the wood cross a macadam drive and take a woodland track straight on, gradu-ally bearing right. On leaving the wood, bear half left across a field to a signposted path through a scrubby box wood, descending a series of steps and then following the contours of Beacon Hill to a kissing-gate. Now take an obvious path across open downland rounding the hill to a kissing-gate, then head for Ellesborough Church to reach a kissing-gate onto the Wendover road opposite a row of thatched cottages.

Turn right along the road, then, at a bus stop, cross the road and take a macadam path (E10a) up a slope to enter the churchyard. Inside the churchyard, leave the macadam path and follow the left-hand wall past the church tower, soon descending a series of steps. Where the steps turn left, leave them and continue straight on through a kissing-gate then steeply downhill to a stile. Cross this and keep straight on across a field to a gate and stile. Do not cross this stile, but instead turn right onto path E16 and follow a left-hand fence crossing two stiles to reach the end of Springs Lane by a cottage. Take this lane (path E14) straight on past several cottages and a farm. Where the lane turns right, leave it bearing slightly right and taking a green lane right of a hydrant (path E13) straight on into a field. Here follow what is usually a crop break to a stile, then continue between fences, crossing three stiles and reaching Chalkshire Road. Turn right onto this road and retrace your steps to your starting point.

Length of Walk: 5.3 miles / 8.5 Km
Starting Point: Clocktower at the northeastern end of
Wendover High Street.
Grid Ref: SP870079
Maps: OS Landranger Sheet 165
OS Explorer Sheet 181 (or old Sheet 2)
Chiltern Society FP Map No.18
Parking: Adequate on- or off-street parking is available in or
near the town centre.
Notes: The descent from Boddington Hill tends to be slippery.

Wendover, an ancient borough on the Upper Icknield Way at one of the few real gaps in the Chiltern escarpment, would seem to be a settlement of considerable antiquity. Not only is it located on an ancient road, but also Iron Age pottery was found here and its name is of Celtic origin deriving from ´Gwyn-dwfr` meaning ´holy` or ´fair water`. Today the centre of the town retains its old world charm thanks to a wealth of Georgian shops and houses as well as a number of older cottages and some fine trees and since the completion of the town's long-awaited bypass, which has reduced through-traffic, visitors have also been better able to appreciate it.

The walk caters for all tastes, leaving Wendover along the towpath of the disused Wendover Arm of the Grand Union Canal (now under restoration) and following it to Halton. It now crosses Halton Park and returns via the wooded heights of Haddington Hill and Boddington Hill with fine views of the Vale of Aylesbury.

Starting from the clocktower at the northeastern end of Wendover High Street, take Aylesbury Road (part of the B4009) for some 300 yards, then, at a mini-roundabout, turn right into Wharf Road. Follow this for about 200 yards, then, just past a school sign, turn left through a gap onto path W12, the towpath of the Wendover Arm Canal at the end of this canal built in the 1790s. Now follow the towpath (later paths HL19, WT36 and HL19 again) along the left bank of the disused canal for 1.7 miles leaving the town behind. After one mile you pass under a road bridge, then, on reaching a second road bridge, the path leads you onto the village street at Halton.

Turn right over the canal bridge and follow the village street to a right-hand bend just past a bus shelter. Here turn left through the gates of Halton churchyard onto path HL3 leading to Halton church, built in 1813. The immaculately maintained churchyard contains a large number of airmen's graves bearing witness to Halton's long-standing and continuing links with the RAF. By the church bear half right and take a macadam path passing right of the church to a kissing-gate at the far side of the churchyard. Go through this gate, then bear half left leaving the concrete path. Passing left of a tall lime tree and the houses ahead, take a path into a belt of trees, keeping left at a fork and continuing to a crossing gravel track. Turn right onto this and follow it through the belt of trees until you emerge onto a macadam drive. Now turn left onto this drive where you may glimpse Halton House, built in 1884 for Baron Alfred de Rothschild in a French chateau style, through the trees to your right and follow the drive through Halton Park for over a third of a mile, later with wide views to your left towards Aylesbury and Waddesdon Manor, another Rothschild mansion, beyond. Where the drive turns sharp right in a wooded area, leave it and bear right onto path AC25, a rough woodland track. After some 250 yards bear half left onto another macadam drive and, ignoring a left-hand turning, follow the drive to the B4009.

Cross this fast road carefully and take a side-road opposite. Where this turns right into a housing estate, go straight on along a rough track (path AC25) to a gate. Ignoring a branching path to the right, pass through a gap by the gate and take the track straight on for half a mile bearing right at a clearing and disregarding all crossing paths. Where the track (now path HL7a) finally forks, bear half right, ignoring a path dropping steeply to the right, and take path HL17, a track hugging the contours of the hill. After a third of a mile, where the track rounds Haddington Hill, fine views open out through the trees to the right towards Coombe Hill and Wendover. 350 yards further on, another track merges from the right. Here take path HL8 straight on for another quarter mile until you reach a gate and gap. Now ignore a branching path to the left and on reaching a turning circle at the end of a Forestry Commission gravel road, keep right of it and take a track (path HL8a) straight on through a gap by a gate. After about 100 yards, where the track forks, bear half right onto a wide path (still HL8a) descending for a quarter mile taking care not to slip on the treacherous chalky surface. At the foot of the hill you emerge from Halton Wood, cross a wide track and keep straight on through a gap by wooden rails. After a few yards bear left onto bridleway W17, a macadam drive, and follow it straight on until you reach a bend in an estate road. Turn right onto this road and follow it to its end. Here turn left into Tring Road and follow it past the 'Rose and Crown' to join the B4009, then turn left onto this for Wendover town centre.

16

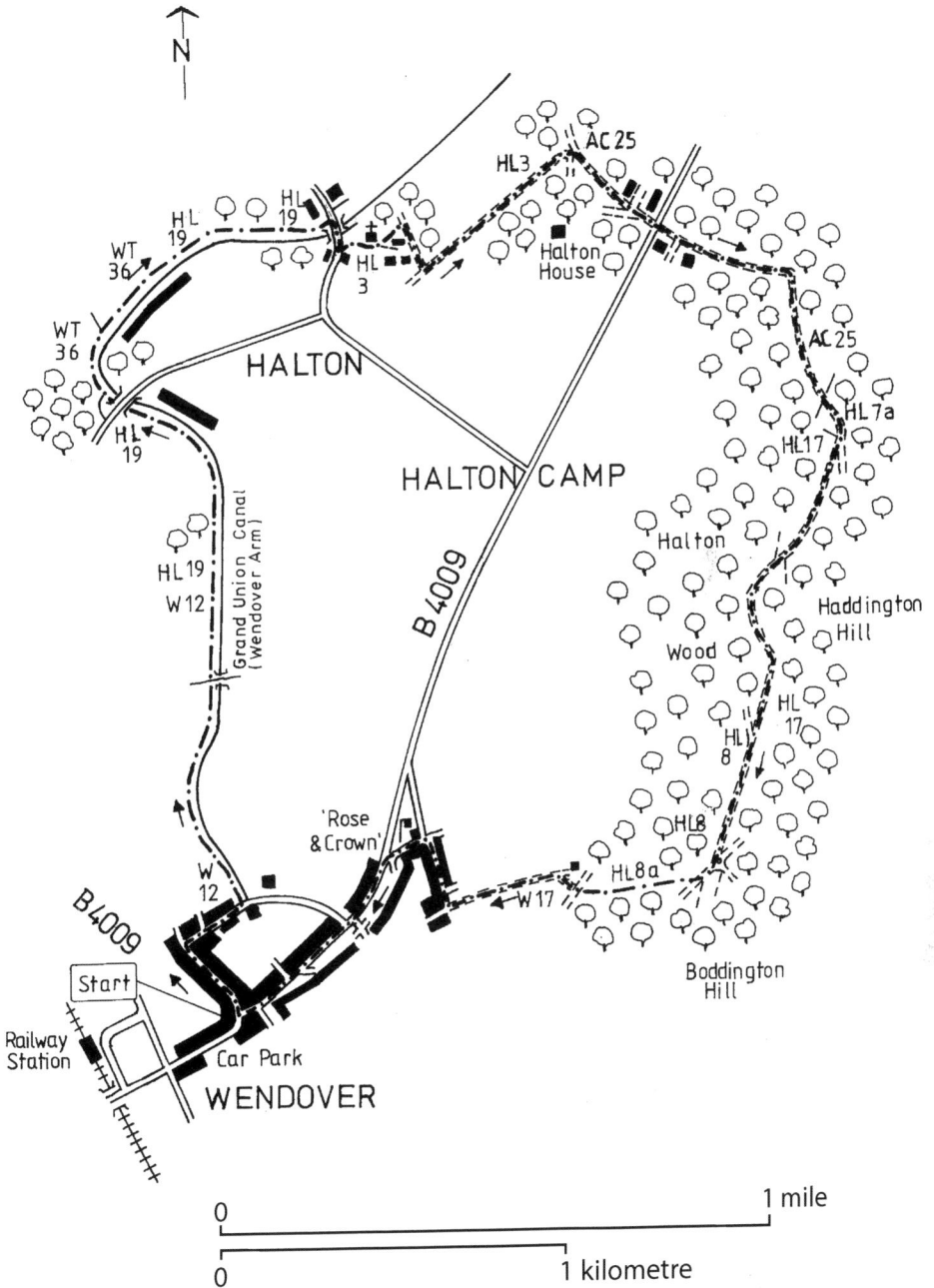

WALK 2

N

WALK 2 map showing route from Wendover through Halton, Halton Camp, Wendover Arm of the Grand Union Canal, and wooded areas including Halton Wood, Haddington Hill, and Boddington Hill.

Map labels:
- AC 25
- HL3
- HL 19
- WT 36
- HL 19
- WT 36
- Halton House
- HL 3
- HALTON
- AC 25
- HL 7a
- HL17
- HL 19
- HALTON CAMP
- Halton
- Haddington Hill
- Grand Union Canal (Wendover Arm)
- HL19 W12
- B4009
- Wood
- HL 17
- HL 8
- 'Rose & Crown'
- HL8
- W 12
- HL8a
- W 17
- Boddington Hill
- B4009
- Start
- Railway Station
- Car Park
- WENDOVER

0 ——————— 1 mile

0 ——————— 1 kilometre

WALK 3   Wendover Woods

Length of Walk: 5.8 miles / 9.4 Km
Starting Point: Entrance to Café in the Wood at central car parking area in Wendover Woods.
Grid Ref: SP889090
Maps: OS Landranger Sheet 165
OS Explorer Sheet 181 (or old Sheet 2)
Chiltern Society FP Map No. 18
How to get there / Parking: Wendover Woods, 1.5 miles north-east of Wendover, may be reached from the town by taking the B4009 towards Tring for 2 miles through Halton, then turning right onto the St. Leonard's, Cholesbury and Chesham road. After 300 yards, after rounding a right-hand bend, turn right onto a one-way Forestry Commission road and follow it for just over a mile to the central car parking area with several small car parks.

Wendover Woods are an extensive area of Forestry Commission woodland to the northeast of Wendover on the highest ridge in the Chilterns. Today these woods are popular due to the recreational facilities provided by the Commission and their excellent network of public and permissive paths. In recognition of its efforts in setting this up, the Commission received a Countryside Award in 1970. In the past, however, the Chiltern woods provided a hide-out for outlaws such as Sir Adam de Gurdon, who was dispossessed of his estates for siding with de Montfort in the Barons War. Tracked down in Wendover Woods by the future King Edward I in 1266, Sir Adam was defeated by Edward in single combat, but is said to have won Edward's admiration for his valour, as a result of which the two became friends.

This walk, as well as traversing a considerable amount of woodland, leads you to Aston Hill with its fine views out into the Vale of Aylesbury, descends the escarpment into farmland near Tring, visits the Hertfordshire hilltop hamlet of Hastoe and returns via the cairn marking the Chiltern summit.

Starting with your back to the entrance to the Café in the Wood, take a gravel path straight ahead, soon reaching a small car park. Here bear slightly left, joining path HL7 and soon joining a Forestry

Commission macadam road. Now follow this (soon on path HL14, later AC39) for a third of a mile. Where the road turns left and starts to descend, take path AC39 straight on at a fork, leaving the macadamed road and passing a padlocked gate. About 50 yards before reaching another gate, turn right onto crossing path AC26 to a stile out of the wood. Cross this and bear half left across a field, keeping left of an old concrete triangulation post to a stile, then ignore a crossing drive and keep straight on to the road at Aston Hill where there are fine views to your left.

Aston Hill, part of the escarpment above Aston Clinton from which it derives its name, marks the northern end of the highest Chiltern ridge. From this vantage point, there is a fine view over Wilstone Reservoir and the Vale of Aylesbury towards Mentmore Towers on its prominent ridge about six miles to the north. This mansion was built for Baron Mayer de Rothschild by Sir Joseph Paxton, designer of the Crystal Palace, in 1852 and was for nearly a century the home of the Earls of Rosebery including a late nineteenth-century prime minister.

Turn left onto this road, then almost immediately right onto path AC13. Follow this gravel drive for a third of a mile, ignoring branching tracks and paths to the left and passing a field to the right to reach the gates to Aston Hill Place. Here go through a fence gap to the left of the gates and follow a right-hand fence through woodland to a squeeze-stile. Now on path BL17, follow a left-hand fence straight on to reach the corner of a field to your left, then, with fine views towards Tring Reservoirs, Mentmore Towers and Ivinghoe Beacon to your left in places, follow the inside edge of the wood known as Buckland Hoo straight on until you reach Dancers End Lane.

Turn right onto this road and just past a left-hand gate turn left onto narrow enclosed path BL18. After 100 yards the path emerges into a field. Here take fenced path DB21 straight on, then, where the fence turns right, follow the left-hand hedge straight on through two fields to reach byway TU36, a green lane following the county boun-dary called Fox Lane. Turn right into this and follow it for a quarter of a mile to reach Duckmore Lane. Having crossed this road, continue straight on along a rough lane (still TU36) to a cottage where it narrows. Now keep straight on for a further third of a mile, ignoring a crossing path (the route of Herts. Walk 10) and later entering Grove Wood. About 80 yards into the wood, by the corner of a right-hand field, turn sharp left onto bridleway TU27, which climbs at first, then levels out as a ledge following the contours of the hill until you reach a T-junction. Here turn sharp right onto restricted byway TU74, a sunken way climbing the hill. At the top ignore branching paths to left and right and leave the wood by a green lane to emerge onto a rough road (byway TU75). Now follow this straight on to a macadam road at Hastoe, the highest settlement in

Hertfordshire.

Turn right onto this road and follow it to a sharp left-hand bend. Here leave the road, bearing slightly right, ignoring a bridleway to your right and going through the smaller of two gates into Pavis Wood. Now follow the Ridgeway (bridleway DB29) straight on. After about 120 yards, where the track forks, take the left-hand option and keep straight on along the inside edge of the wood, ignoring branching paths to your right. After a third of a mile, at a signposted crossways, (where you recross Herts. Walk 10), take bridleway BL24 straight on along the inside edge of Northill Wood for a quarter of a mile, eventually keeping left at a fork to reach a road at the top of a hill known as The Crong. Turn left onto this road, leaving the woodland. After a few yards, opposite double gates, turn right through a kissing-gate at the left-hand corner of the entrance to a farm track, then take path AC18, crossing a field diagonally to a kissing-gate at the right-hand corner of a small copse of tall conifers in the hollow ahead. Go through this kissing-gate and follow the edge of the copse, later a left-hand hedge, to a kissing-gate leading onto a road by one of the scattered cottages at Chivery.

Cross this road and take bridleway AC42 opposite into Hengrove Wood. At a fork keep right, taking bridleway W47 descending into a sunken way. At a left-hand bend, some 25 yards beyond a signposted path junction to your left, turn right up a sunken gully to cross a mossy boundary bank, then turn right onto a permissive path, following the right-hand boundary bank for some 300 yards to a bend in the Forestry Commission road. Take this road (path HL15) straight on through Halton Wood for over half a mile, then ignore two waymarked paths to your right at a left-hand bend. Now on path HL11, some 75 yards further on, turn right onto a wide winding permissive path. At a T-junction, turn right for a few yards to visit the Chiltern Summit Cairn erected in 1977 to mark the Queen's Silver Jubilee at the highest point in the Chilterns which is 876 feet or 267 metres above sea-level. Now retrace your steps to the T-junction, then keep straight on to reach the main car park in Wendover Woods, where your starting point is to the left.

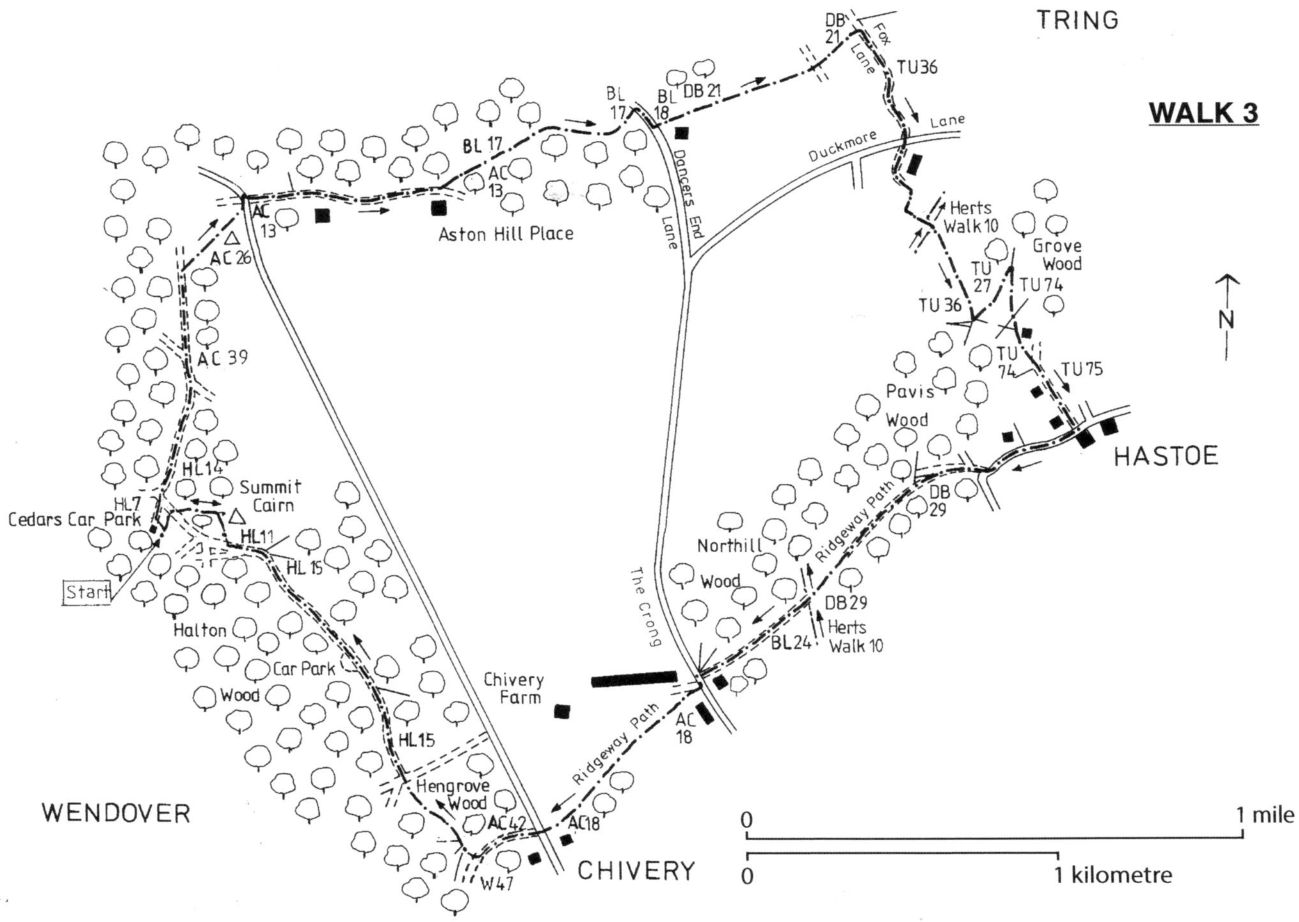

WENDOVER

TRING

WALK 3

Start

Cedars Car Park

HL7

HL16

AC 39

AC 26

AC 13

Summit Cairn

Halton Wood

Car Park

HL11

HL5

HL15

Hengrove Wood

AC 42

W47

AC 18

CHIVERY

Chivery Farm

Ridgeway Path

The Crong

AC 18

Aston Hill Place

BL 17

AC 13

BL 17 18

BL DB21

Dancers End Lane

Duckmore Lane

DB 21

Fox Lane

TU36

Northill Wood

BL 24

DB 29

Herts Walk 10

Ridgeway Path

Pavis Wood

TU36

TU 27

TU 74

TU74

TU75

Grove Wood

Herts Walk 10

HASTOE

N →

0

0

1 kilometre

1 mile

21

WALK 4	The Lee

Length of Walk: 5.5 miles / 8.8 Km
Starting Point: ´Cock & Rabbit`, The Lee village green.
Grid Ref: SP900042
Maps: OS Landranger Sheet 165
OS Explorer Sheet 181 (or old Sheet 2)
Chiltern Society FP Maps Nos. 3 & 8

How to get there / Parking: The Lee, 3 miles southeast of
Wendover, may be reached from the town by joining and
taking the A413 towards Great Missenden, then turning left
onto a road signposted to Kingsash and The Lee. Follow this
winding lane for nearly two miles, then one-third of a mile
past ´The Gate`, turn right at a crossroads and take a winding
road for three-quarters of a mile to The Lee village green.
Cars may be parked along the road on the southern (right-
hand) side of the green, which is not used by through-traffic,
but should not block the road or driveways. Do not use the
pub car park without the landlord's permission.

The Lee is both a collective name for a group of isolated hamlets and
the particular name of one. Situated on a hilltop plateau above the
Misbourne valley and connected to the outside world only by narrow
winding lanes, The Lee proper with its pub, manor house and a few
cottages around its pleasant village green, is a secluded haven of
rural life. One surprising feature of the village is that it has two
churches. The older one, of thirteenth-century origin, was replaced
by the nearby brick structure in 1868, but was retained as a Sunday
school and has since been restored. Both churches and nearby
Church Farm stand within the bounds of an ancient camp, a circular
earthwork, and this would suggest early habitation of the area. In
more recent times, the village manor house was purchased in 1900
by Sir Arthur Lasenby Liberty, the founder of Liberty's department
store in London's Regent Street, who proved a considerable
benefactor to the village and whose descendants still live locally.

The walk takes you first through the ancient camp between the
churches and Church Farm, then through open country, descending
with fine views into the dry upper reaches of the Misbourne valley at
Wendover Dean. The heights are subsequently regained at Kingsash
before you circle through a heavily-wooded area on and above the

Chiltern escarpment to reach Swan Bottom and return to The Lee.

Starting from the 'Cock and Rabbit' at The Lee village green, take the side-road westwards around the southern side of the green. At the far end of the green, take the winding road out of the village past the new church. Just past the far end of the churchyard, turn left over a stile onto path L48 following a left-hand hedge concealing the old church to a gate and stile between Church Farm and a cottage. Here cross the stile, the drive to the cottage and a further stile and then take path L4 bearing half right across a field to a gate and stile. Cross the stile onto a track and, after a few yards, turn left onto a crossing track and follow a left-hand hedge for a third of a mile to a stile into King's Lane, onto which you turn left. At a road junction, ignore Bowwood Lane branching to the right and turn right onto path L3, a track into a wood which runs parallel to Bowwood Lane. Where the track bears left away from the road, leave the track and follow the inside edge of the wood straight on beside the road to a gap into a field where wide views of the Misbourne valley open out ahead. Go through this gap and take path W37, following a right-hand hedge straight on downhill, passing under a power line and through a hedge gap. After a third of a mile, on reaching a gap in the right-hand hedge with a double-armed footpath signpost, bear right through this gap and join Bowwood Lane. Take this road for a further third of a mile to a road junction just past Wendoverdean Farm.

Here go straight on along a 'no through road', following it round a sharp right-hand bend. At a second sharp right-hand bend, turn left into a hedged lane (path W39) and follow it winding uphill for 250 yards. Where the main track bears right into a field, turn right into a right-hand field and take path W40, following a left-hand hedge, later a belt of trees. Beyond the belt of trees, where the hedge turns left, follow its winding course, gradually climbing to reach a stile at the far end of the field. Cross this stile onto path L9, then, keeping just right of the bottom of the combe, continue straight on uphill, heading towards a house to the right of one with large windows, to reach a kissing-gate leading to King's Lane near a road junction at Kingsash.

Turn left onto this road and at the road junction, turn left again. After about 130 yards, by Robertswood Cottage, turn right into a rough lane (bridleway L45). Just past the cottage, leave the lane and take fenced path W35 on the other side of the lane's left-hand hedge. Now follow this path through woodland for over half a mile until it eventually drops down to rejoin the parallel bridleway L45. Just beyond this, on reaching a track (bridleway L11, part of the Ridgeway), turn right onto it. At a fork, keep left, following the Ridgeway waymarks, then, at a second fork, take the waymarked bridleway forking right and follow it climbing steadily for a third of a mile. Where it levels out, look out for a signposted junction.

Here turn right, leaving the Ridgeway and taking narrow woodland path L11, which gradually swings to the left and reaches a crossing track. Turn left onto this track and at three subsequent forks, keep straight on, ignoring a branching track to the left and two to the right. On reaching a mature plantation, keep right, following its right-hand edge, then at its corner, continue straight on, ignoring two crossing tracks and bearing slightly right. Now go straight on through Great Widmoor Wood, passing a triangulation post and disregarding several crossing tracks. On passing a field to your left, ignore a wide crossing bridleway known as Timberley Lane, then continue through Lordling Wood for a further quarter mile. Just before reaching a rough road and some sheds, bear half left, **crossing the route of Walk 5** and take path L11 through some hollybushes, ignoring a wicket-gate to your right and continuing past the backs of several cottages to reach a squeeze-stile by the corner of a field. Go through this squeeze-stile and follow the right-hand hedge of an overgrown orchard, later diverging from the hedge and taking a grass garden path to pass right of a black wooden garage and left of a cottage to reach gates onto a road some 130 yards north of the ´Old Swan`.

Turn right onto this road, then almost immediately left over a stile opposite the cottages onto path L19. Now follow a right-hand hedge to cross a stile by a gate, then continue through two further paddocks to reach a gate and stile. Cross this stile and turn right onto path L18b, **joining Walk 5** and the Chiltern Way and following a right-hand hedge to a stile. Having crossed this, take bridleway L18a straight on downhill along an old green lane, **leaving Walk 5** and the Chiltern Way and continuing to two bridlegates onto a road in Swan Bottom.

Go through these gates, cross the road and take a gravel drive opposite (path L18), soon crossing a stile by a gate. Now ignoring a branch to the right, continue along the drive to its end, then follow a left-hand hedge straight on, crossing four stiles before entering a belt of trees. In the trees, turn left onto a track (path L16) and follow it for some 200 yards to a fork. Here fork right onto obvious path L27 through a wood called Old Plantation to a stile. Cross the stile and follow a right-hand hedge to a gate and stile. Having crossed the stile, bear half right up a hedged lane and past a converted barn to a further stile. Cross this and go straight on through a small copse past a pond to a road at The Lee where you turn right for the village green.

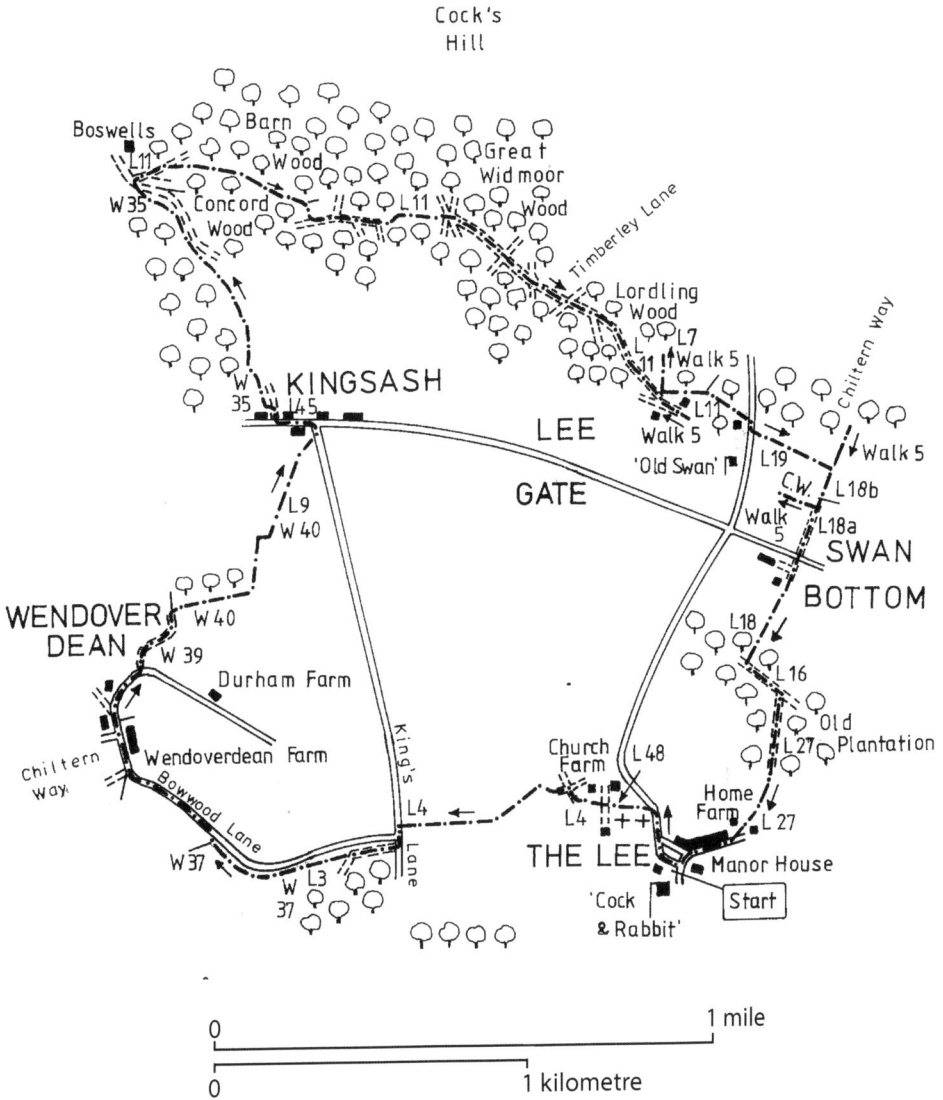

WALK 4

Cock's Hill

Boswells
Barn Wood
L11
W35
Concord Wood
Great Widmoor Wood
L11
Timberley Lane
Lordling Wood
L7
Walk 5
L11
W 35
KINGSASH
L45
LEE
GATE
Old Swan
Walk 5
Walk 5
L19
L18b
C.W.
Walk 5
L18a
Chiltern Way
Walk 5
SWAN
BOTTOM
L9
W 40
WENDOVER DEAN
W 40
W 39
Durham Farm
L18
L16
Old Plantation
L27
Chiltern Way
Wendoverdean Farm
Bowwood Lane
King's Lane
Church Farm
L48
Home Farm
L27
L4
L4
THE LEE
Manor House
W 37
W 37
L3
Cock & Rabbit
Start

0   1 mile

0   1 kilometre

25

WALK 5   Cholesbury

Length of Walk: 7.3 miles / 11.8 Km
Starting Point: Cholesbury Village Hall.
Grid Ref: SP930071
Maps: OS Landranger Sheet 165
OS Explorer Sheet 181 (or old Sheet 2)
Chiltern Society FP Maps Nos. 3 & 8
How to get there / Parking: Cholesbury, 4 miles northwest of
Chesham, may be reached from the town by taking the A416
northwards. At a sharp right-hand bend, leave the A416 and
continue straight on along a road signposted to Cholesbury
and Hawridge (**not** Bellingdon), following it for 3.7 miles to
Cholesbury Common. The village hall is on the right about
150 yards past a turning signposted to Tring. Cars can be
parked along the edge of the common.
Notes: Due, in part, to the remote nature of the area, some paths
are in poor condition and difficult to follow. Also heavy
nettle growth may be encountered in places in summer.

Cholesbury is probably best known today for its picturesque windmill, a tower mill originally constructed as a smock mill in 1863 but
rebuilt in its present form in 1884. With its cottages scattered around
its spacious common, it is one of the most unspoilt villages in the
Bucks Chilterns and forms the gateway to some of their most remote
country. The village is also an ancient settlement, as its thirteenth-
century church, largely rebuilt in 1872-3, stands within a ten-feet-
high Iron Age camp enclosing fifteen acres of land and its Saxon
name of ´Ceolweald's burh` confirms that the camp existed at that
time. Originally a hilltop hamlet of Drayton Beauchamp parish,
whose mother village is 3.5 miles to the northwest in the Vale of
Aylesbury, following the construction of Cholesbury Church as a
chapel-of-ease, the village, at some time, became a separate parish.
In 1932, the civil parish was amalgamated with neighbouring
Hawridge and the remaining upland areas of the Vale parishes of
Drayton Beauchamp, Buckland and Aston Clinton to form the
modern hilltop parish of Cholesbury-cum-St. Leonard's.
    The walk explores the remote, heavily-wooded hill country to the
west of Cholesbury, skirting Lee Gate before descending the escarpment at The Hale, where there are superb views of the Wendover

Gap. It then returns by a more northerly route, passing close to St. Leonard's and Buckland Common. Despite the difficult conditions sometimes encountered, the walk is scenically most rewarding.

Starting from Cholesbury Village Hall, take the road westwards, then, almost immediately, turn left onto path CY44 left of the Old Rectory, taking a fenced path by the near end of a wooden fence to a kissing-gate. Here follow a left-hand fence straight on downhill to pass through another kissing-gate. Now turn right onto path CY19 beside a right-hand fence passing through a further kissing-gate, then follow a right-hand hedge straight on through two fields to a tree belt at the far end of the second field. Here turn left onto path CY12, following the edge of the tree belt. Where, after some 30 yards, the tree belt bears away to the right, leave it, heading for the left-hand end of a row of tall poplars on the skyline to reach Oak Lane by the end of a hedge.

Turn right onto this road and at a sharp right-hand bend, leave it and take path CY17a over a stile left of a private road, joining the road just beyond the gates of a wood called Widow Croft. About 30 yards beyond the gates, fork right onto the second right-hand track. Halfway across the wood at a fork, keep right, then later ignore a crossing track and continue to the far corner of the wood. Here, joining path CY15, follow a left-hand hedge for about 70 yards to a gap in it, then turn left through the gap and take path CY17, heading for the left-hand end of the buildings at Dundridge Manor. Continue past the buildings, then bear half right to reach a concrete road (path CY8). Turn right onto this, immediately bearing left and keeping left of the buildings, then continue past a large duckpond to your right.

Where the road turns right, leave it and, joining the Chiltern Way, turn left into a wide, ancient green lane (bridleway CY6), following it downhill to reach a wood called Ashen Grove. Where the lane bears right and enters the wood, leave it and take path CY46 straight on beside a left-hand hedge into a field. Here go straight on uphill to enter a wood called Lady Grove by a gap right of a tall ash tree, then keep straight on through the wood, passing between a green shed and a shallow pit and descending to reach an obvious crossing path in the valley bottom. Cross this and continue straight on through a hedge gap into a field, then aim to pass just right of a clump of trees on the skyline to reach a hedge gap leading to Arrewig Lane.

Turn right onto this road, then, after about 50 yards, turn left through a hedge gap onto path L18b, following a right-hand hedge downhill. Where three hedges meet in the valley bottom, go straight on through a gap between the other two and bear slightly right across the field, passing over a rise to reach a hedge gap with a marker post into a strip of woodland. In the wood, go straight on, crossing it diagonally to a stile.

Cross this and follow a right-hand hedge uphill through two fields, **joining the route of Walk 4**. At the far side of the second field, cross a stile by a gate, then, after some 10 yards, **leaving Walk 4** again, turn right over a stile onto path L20a. Now follow a right-hand line of trees, later a left-hand fence, to reach a gate and stile onto a road near the ´Old Swan`.

Turn right onto the road, then immediately left into a flint lane left of the pub (byway L43) and follow it, (soon leaving the Chiltern Way), until you enter Lordling Wood. Here turn right into the wood and take path L7, the central option of a three-way fork, **recrossing the route of Walk 4** and following this waymarked path straight on through the wood. On emerging into a field, bear half left to cross a bridleway and sporadic hedge line just right of the bottom of a dip, then bear slightly right across the next field, with a view over your right shoulder towards Chesham to reach a hedge gap right of a Scots pine into Baldwin's Wood.

In the wood, ignore a crossing path and take path W43 straight on through a squeeze-stile into a plantation. Where the path forks, bear slightly left, soon entering a field. Go straight on across the field to a hedge gap, then take a grassy track through the corner of a wood and along its outside edge. Soon the track passes through another strip of woodland, where a pronounced section of the ancient earthwork known as Grim's Ditch is visible in the trees to your left. On emerging into a field, where the track turns right, leave it and bear slightly right across the field to the near corner of an area of scrub, then follow its left-hand edge to the right-hand end of a brick wall by a gate. Here pass through a V-stile and keep straight on past Uphill Farm, soon entering Hale Wood, passing a redundant gate and ignoring a waymarked crossing path, to reach the Ridgeway. Cross this and take a sunken path straight on downhill. At a crossways near the bottom edge of the wood, bear half right, ignoring the crossing path, then leave the wood by a stile and head for a gate in the bottom corner of the field. Go through this gate and turn left into Hale Lane, passing the sixteenth-century Hale Farmhouse and Hale Barn at The Hale.

Just past Hale Barn, turn right onto signposted bridleway W47. On entering Halton Wood, turn right onto path W42 up a flight of steps and over a stile, then turn left onto a track into a field. Now follow the outside edge of Halton Wood straight on until you reach a wooden pylon. Here bear slightly right, leaving the edge of the wood and walking under a powerline to pass through a small gate and soon reach a fence gap into another wood by the next pylon. Here turn round to admire the superb view towards The Hale and Bacombe Hill, before continuing steeply uphill through the wood under the power-line. Near the top of the hill, you recross the Ridgeway, leave the wood by a stile and turn left along

WALK 5

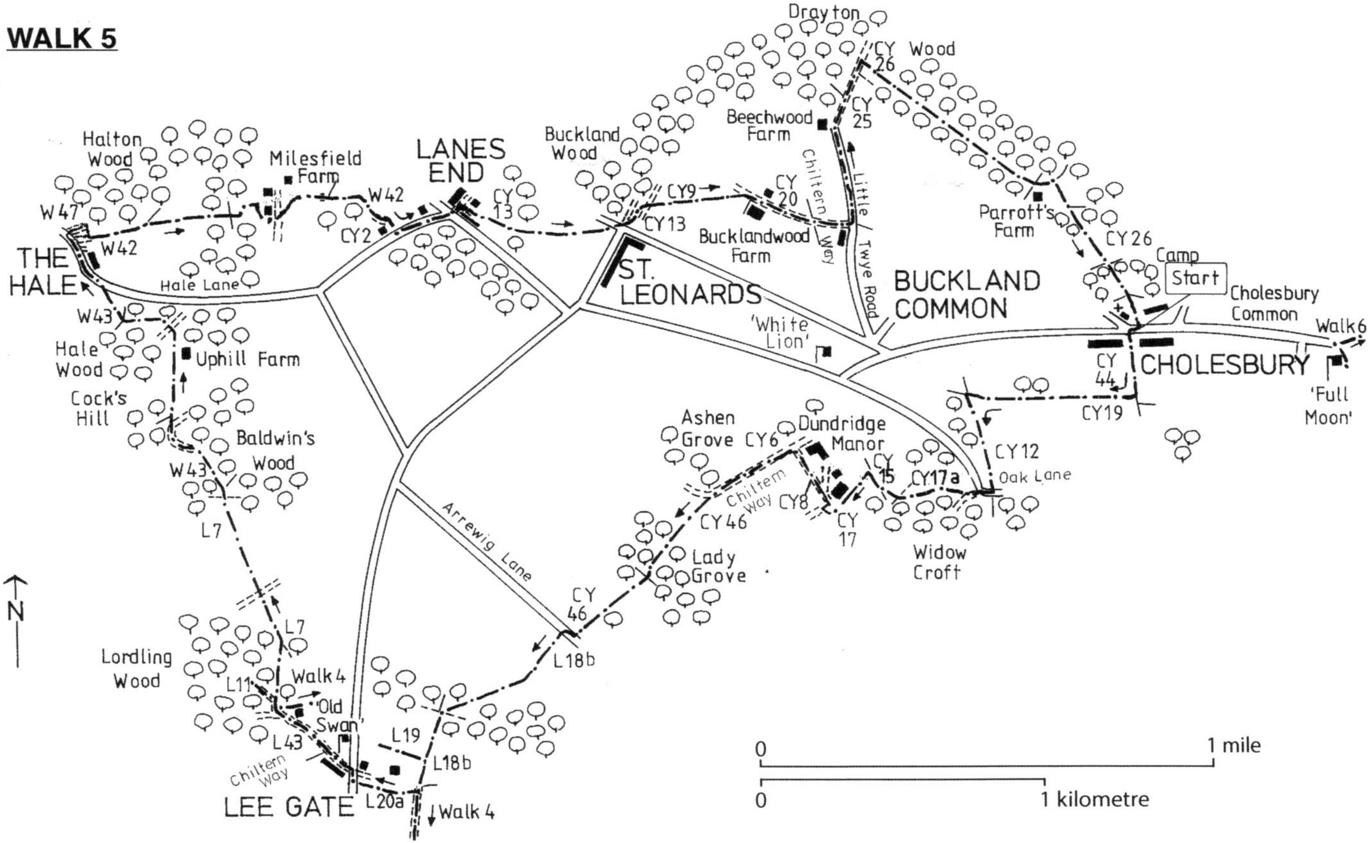

N→

THE HALE

W47
W42
W43
Hale Lane

Halton Wood
Hale Wood
Cock's Hill
Milesfield Farm
Baldwin's Wood
Uphill Farm
Lordling Wood
W43
L7
L7
L7
L11
L43
Chiltern Way
'Old Swan'
Walk4
LEE GATE
L20a
L19
L18b
L18b
CY 46
Arrewig Lane
Walk 4

CY2
W42
LANES END
CY 13
CY13
CY9
Buckland Wood
ST. LEONARDS
Buckland-wood Farm
CY 20
Beechwood Farm
Drayton Wood
CY 25
CY 26
Chiltern Way
Little 'Twye Road
'White Lion'
Ashen Grove CY6
Dundridge Manor
Lady Grove
CY8
CY 17
CY 46
Chiltern Way
CY 15
CY17a
Widow Croft
Oak Lane
CY12
BUCKLAND COMMON
Parrott's Farm
CY 44
CY19
Camp Start
Cholesbury Common
CHOLESBURY
'Full Moon'
Walk 6

0

0
1 kilometre

0
1 mile

29

a fenced path, following the edge of the wood, then a left-hand hedge. At Milesfield Farm, ignore a gate ahead and bear half right between a hedge and a fence to cross a concrete drive flanked by stiles. Now bear slightly left across the next field to a gate and stile. Cross the stile, then, where the hedge turns left, bear slightly right to cross a stile by a concealed gate in the far right-hand corner of the field. Now take an old green lane straight on, soon with a garden fence to your right. Where the lane narrows to an enclosed path, take path CY2 along it, bearing right to a road at Lanes End. Turn left onto the road and at a junction, pass the right-hand side of the grass triangle, cross the priority road and take the drive into Coppice Farm Park (path CY13). Now take the first turning right, then bear half left across a car park to a kissing-gate. Here go straight on across a field to a kissing-gate left of the last mobile home. Now keep straight on, heading for a modern red-brick house right of the end of Buckland Wood to reach a hedge gap, then bear slightly left across the next field to a stile just left of the bottom corner of the field leading to a road junction on the edge of St. Leonard's. Now cross the road and go through a kissing-gate by a gate opposite into Buckland Wood. Inside the wood, where the track forks, take the right-hand path along the inside edge of the wood, looking out for a stile to your right into a field. On reaching it, turn right over it onto path CY9, then bear half left across the field, heading just left of Bucklandwood Farm to reach the far corner of the field. Here take path CY20, crossing a stile by a gate and following a lane through the farm and on for a quarter mile to Little Twye Road on the edge of Buckland Common.

Turn left onto this road and follow it to its end by a cottage. Here take a gravel lane (bridleway CY25) straight on, soon with Drayton Wood on your left, ignoring a stile and later a gate in the left-hand fence. Where the right-hand field ends, cross a stile in the right-hand fence onto path CY26 and follow its winding course along the inside edge of Drayton Wood for half a mile until you reach a stile to your right leading out of the wood. Ignore this stile and continue straight on, gradually bearing left until you reach a second right-hand stile. Turn right over this (still on path CY26) and follow a right-hand hedge, passing through a kissing-gate to reach a stile into Tomlin's Wood, then go straight on along the inside edge of this wood to a stile. Now take an obvious path straight on through an area of scrub to a gap in the high banks and ditch of Cholesbury's Iron Age camp. Here cross the camp ditch and a stile by a gate and follow a slightly sunken track straight on across a field to cross a stile by a gate between two oaks, then bear slightly right to a gate and stile. Cross the stile and take a track straight on to reach Cholesbury Common by the side of the village hall.

WALK 6   Hawridge Common

Length of Walk: 7.9 miles / 12.8 Km
Starting Point: 'Full Moon', Hawridge Common.
Grid Ref: SP936070
Maps: OS Landranger Sheet 165
          OS Explorer Sheet 181 (or old Sheet 2)
          Chiltern Society FP Map No.8
How to get there / Parking: Hawridge Common, 3.5 miles
    northwest of Chesham, may be reached from the town by
    taking the A416 northwards. At a sharp right-hand bend,
    leave the A416 and continue straight on along a road
    signposted to Cholesbury and Hawridge (**not** Bellingdon),
    following it for 3.4 miles to the 'Full Moon' at Hawridge
    Common, where cars can be parked along the edge of the
    common.
Notes: Heavy nettle growth may be encountered in the summer
    in several places.

Hawridge (pronounced 'Harridge') and its neighbour Cholesbury today form a long sporadic ribbon along a ridgetop road with most of their buildings on the south side and their twin commons on the north side. Their boundary just west of the 'Full Moon' can only be perceived by virtue of the back-to-back nameboards marking it. The original site of Hawridge village, which is visited in the course of the walk, is, however, over a mile to the southeast of the 'Full Moon' and consists of the church with its wooden bellcote built in 1856 to replace a thirteenth-century building on the same site, from which the thirteenth-century font remains; timber-framed Hawridge Court with its deep moat, which has been filled in front of the house, and a former farm.

The walk explores the country to the south of Hawridge with its succession of typical Chiltern ridges and bottoms and visits the ridgetop villages of Bellingdon, Asheridge and Chartridge. All these villages and the roads which serve them are located on the ridges as the valleys were formerly marshy. Hence the paths used in this walk were vital means of communication between the various ridges. Although the walk is hilly, its scenery makes the effort well worthwhile.

WALK 6

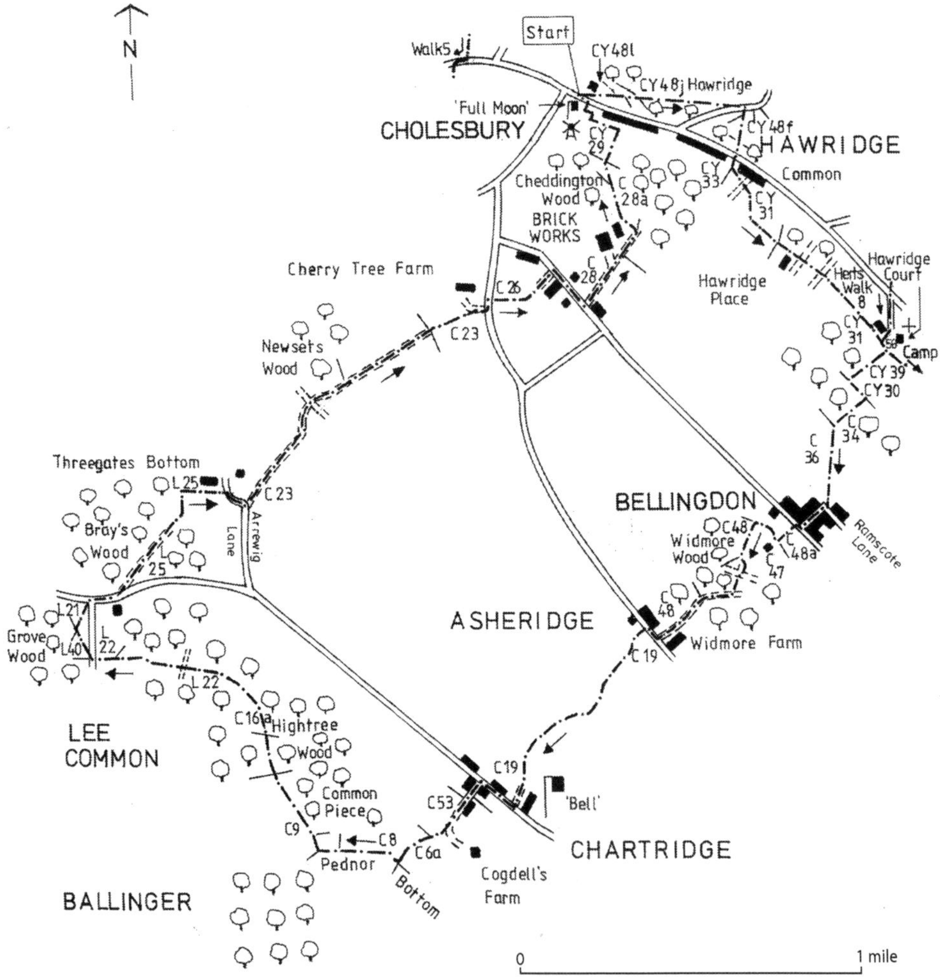
N
Start
Walk5
CY48l
CY48j Hawridge
'Full Moon'
CHOLESBURY
CY 29
CY48f
HAWRIDGE
Common
CY 33
CY 31
Cheddington Wood
C 28a
BRICK WORKS
Cherry Tree Farm
C 26
C 28
Hawridge Place
Hawridge Court
Herts Walk 8
CY 31
Camp
CY 39
CY 30
C 34
C 36
Newsets Wood
C 23
Threegates Bottom
L 25
C 23
Bray's Wood
L 25
Arrewig Lane
BELLINGDON
Ramscote Lane
C48
Widmore Wood
C 48a
C 47
C 48
Widmore Farm
ASHERIDGE
C 19
L 21
Grove Wood
L40
L 22
L 22
C 16a
Hightree Wood
LEE COMMON
C19
'Bell'
Common Piece
C53
C9
C8
C6a
Pednor
Bottom
Cogdell's Farm
CHARTRIDGE
BALLINGER
0
1 mile
0
1 kilometre

Starting from the 'Full Moon' on Hawridge Common, cross the road and turn right onto path CY48l along the verge passing Mermaid Cottage. Just after its garden hedge ends, fork left onto a lesser path. By a deer warning sign and a pair of small oaks, turn left onto an ill-defined path downhill into a large clearing. Here bear left to its bottom edge, then turn right onto a crossing path, eventually reaching a fork in another clearing. Keep left at this fork to join a more prominent parallel track to your left (CY48j). Now follow this track along the valley bottom through an open heathland area for a third of a mile to reach a road. Turn right onto this road, then immediately left onto heathland path CY48f, soon bearing right at a fork, climbing and ignoring three crossing paths to reach the top road right of 'Hill View', opposite signposted path CY33.

Take this path straight on through scrubland to reach an electricity pole at the corner of a hedge. Here turn left onto path CY31, generally following the left-hand hedge, eventually crossing a track and keeping left of a wooden shed. Now bear half right across an overgrown field to a stile. Cross this stile and another stile by a gate, then bear left and follow a left-hand hedge to a stile in the corner of the field. Having crossed this stile, ignore a stile to the left and follow a left-hand fence straight on across a field to a gate and stile. Cross the stile and keep straight on between a hedge and a belt of trees, crossing a stile, the drive to Hawridge Place and another stile, eventually passing through a kissing-gate into a sunken lane. Having crossed a stile opposite, keep straight on across a field, following a powerline, later a left-hand hedge to a stile by gates. Cross the stile and keep straight on past a former farm, at the far side of which path CY56 to your left enables you to make a detour to look at the church and Hawridge Court.

Otherwise, **having briefly joined Herts. Walk 8**, at the far end of the field by a copse concealing the deep moat of Hawridge Court, turn right onto path CY39 and follow a left-hand hedge downhill over a stile to a gate and stile. Cross the stile and bear half right across the corner of a field to a gate by a cattle trough. Go through this, then turn left over high rails and follow a left-hand hedge downhill into a belt of trees. Here turn left over a stile on path CY30 and follow the belt of trees to a pair of right-hand stiles. Turn right over these and take path C34, following a right-hand fence uphill to a gap in the top hedge. Go through this and take path C36, bearing half left across a field and passing the corner of a hedge to reach a gate and gap in the far corner of the field. Here turn right into Ramscote Lane and follow it into Bellingdon.

On reaching the main village road, turn right. After 40 yards, turn left through a kissing-gate and take path C48a beside a right-hand hedge to a hedge gap in the corner of the field. Here turn right through a kissing-gate onto path C47, following a right-hand hedge to a former gateway. Do **not** go through this, but turn left onto path C48 and follow a right-hand hedge downhill to a stile into Widmore Wood. Having crossed this, fork left, then turn left onto a crossing track. Now turn immediately right and follow a path downhill to a crossing track in the valley bottom. Cross this track and bear half left uphill, joining one track, ignoring a crossing path and joining another track, eventually leaving the top of the wood by a concrete road. Follow this straight on to green gates at Widmore Farm, then bear half right, passing right of the farmhouse to reach a road at Asheridge.

Turn right onto this road and after about 90 yards, turn left through a kissing-gate, taking path C19 beside a right-hand hedge downhill. Where the hedge turns right, leave it and keep straight on to a hedge gap on the other side of the valley, then follow a left-hand hedge straight on uphill. At the top corner of the field, keep straight on into a hedged path and follow it for a quarter mile. On emerging into a field, follow the left-hand hedge, then a rough lane, straight on to a road at Chartridge.

Turn right onto this road and after about 200 yards, turn left into Cogdells Lane. Follow this straight on to the end of its macadam surface, then take bridleway C53 straight on along a rough lane. Where this lane forks, bear half right and where the lane turns right, take path C6a straight on over a stile by a gate, following a left-hand hedge downhill to a stile in Pednor Bottom. Cross the stile and turn right onto bridleway C8 between a hedge and a fence, later a wood called Common Piece and a fence, and follow this along the valley bottom for a quarter mile, ignoring a branching path into the wood. Where Bellows Wood begins to the left, turn right onto bridleway C9 along the inside edge of Common Piece. After a quarter mile, go straight on through a kissing-gate onto path C16a and follow it straight on for over half a mile through Hightree Wood and Lownde's Wood, disregarding all branching paths until you leave the wood by a kissing-gate. Here take path L22 straight on across a field to a gate and stile, then follow a right-hand fence straight on to a kissing-gate onto a road near Lee Common.

Now enter Grove Wood opposite, then bear half right following waymarked path L40 for about 140 yards to a waymarked crossways. Here turn right and take waymarked path L21 to a road junction. Now turn right onto the major road and follow it for about 250 yards. At the start of Bray's Wood to the left, turn left over a stile and bear half right, following the ill-defined but waymarked path L25 across the wood to a stile leading out into a field. Now bear half left to the bottom corner of the field, then turn right and follow a left-hand hedge to a stile into Arrewig Lane at Threegates Bottom.

Cross the stile and turn right onto the road. At a right-hand bend, turn left and take bridleway C23, following a track beside a left-hand hedge over a hill. Where the track transfers to the other side of the hedge, continue to follow it. Near the top of the hill, ignore a branching track to your right, then, at a fork, go right, transferring back to the right-hand side of the hedge. Just past Newsets Wood, where the track forks, bear slightly right with a copse to your left and a hedge to your right, then, on entering a field, follow the right-hand hedge straight on for a quarter mile until you enter the next field. Here continue straight on across the field to a bridlegate. Go through this gate and bear slightly left to a gate at Cherry Tree Farm, then take a gravel drive past the farm to a road. Turn left onto the road and after 50 yards, turn right over a stile and take path C26 straight across a field to cross another stile under an oak tree. Now bear half left, heading for the left-hand corner of a farm compound. Having crossed a stile here, join a concrete drive and follow it straight on out to a road

Turn right onto the road and after about 200 yards, turn left onto path C28, the macadam drive to a brickworks. At the brickworks, cross a stile by gates, then fork right to pass the right-hand side of the showroom building. Now ignore a stile to your right and keep straight on over a stile by gates, then follow a right-hand hedge to the back of the works. Here turn left over a stile onto path C28a and follow a right-hand hedge, crossing another stile and entering Cheddington Wood. Now follow the inside edge of the wood downhill, ignoring a branching path to the left, to reach a stile at the bottom. Cross this stile, ignore a stile to the right and keep straight on to cross a further stile onto path CY29. Now follow a right-hand hedge uphill to a gate in the top corner of the field. Do **not** go through this, but turn left and follow a right-hand fence to a stile, then keep straight on to a stile in the right-hand hedge, with a good view ahead of Cholesbury Windmill, a tower mill originally constructed as a smock mill in 1863 but rebuilt in its present form in 1884. Now turn right over this stile and take a fenced path. Where a hedge blocks the way ahead, turn left through a hedge gap and follow the right-hand hedge to a gate and stile. Here turn right for your starting point.

WALK 7   Ashley Green

Length of Walk: 6.1 miles / 9.9 Km
Starting Point: Ashley Green Village Hall.
Grid Ref: SP977051
Maps: OS Landranger Sheet 165
OS Explorer Sheet 181 (or old Sheet 2)
Chiltern Society FP Map No.17
How to get there / Parking: Ashley Green, two miles south of
Berkhamsted and two and a half miles north of Chesham,
may be reached from either town by taking the A416
towards the other town. By Ashley Green Church, turn off
the main road into Two Dells Lane, signposted to Bovingdon,
and after 150 yards, turn left into the village hall car park.
Notes: Heavy nettle growth may be encountered in the summer
in several places.

Despite its suburban appearance, Ashley Green, situated on a hilltop
plateau between the Chess and Bulbourne valleys, is a good centre
for walking in the surrounding countryside. Much of this walk is of
an easy nature, exploring the upland plateau to the east and south of
Ashley Green and visiting Whelpley Hill and Lye Green. In the later
stages of the walk there is a magnificent view of Chesham Vale and
the hills beyond and the walk takes you down into the Vale before
reascending to Ashley Green.

Starting from the back of Ashley Green Village Hall car park, pass
between bollards into a recreation ground called Glebe Meadow and bear
half left across it to a kissing-gate in its far left-hand corner. Now take a
fenced permissive path straight on to a gate and kissing-gate. Turn right
through the kissing-gate onto fenced path AG7, turning left, then
ignoring a stile ahead and turning right. At the far end of the right-hand
field, pass through another kissing-gate and follow the left-hand hedge
straight on. Where the hedge ends, turn right onto a fenced track. On
emerging into a field, bear slightly left over a hill to an electricity pylon
and stile in the hedge just beyond it. Cross this stile and bear half left
across a field, passing the right-hand end of a belt of trees to reach a gate
and stile leading into a second belt of trees. Inside this tree belt, take
bridleway AG7b straight on uphill for some 200 yards to Sale's Farm.
Here take path AG7c straight on between a hedge and a fence to a stile,

36

then keep straight on across a large field, passing left of a midfield electricity pole to reach a gap in the far hedge. Here ignore a crossing track and take a fenced path straight on between fields, then through a mobile home park, crossing three site roads and eventually emerging at a road junction at Whelpley Hill.

Turn right here into Grove Lane and follow it round a sharp right-hand bend. Shortly after this bend, turn left through a hedge gap by an overgrown stile onto path AG10 and go straight on across a field to the corner of a hedge. Here follow a left-hand hedge straight on. Where the hedge bears right, go through a gap in it and follow the other side of the hedge, later the outside edge of Bush Wood, straight on to a hedge gap by the far end of this copse. Go through this gap, then cross a bridleway and stile and keep straight on across a field to an electricity pole. Now bear slightly right to reach gates and stiles by the corner of a hedge. Here cross both stiles and another bridleway and continue straight on beside a right-hand fence to a point near the corner of a cottage garden where it bears slightly left and leads you to a gate and stile onto the B4505 at Orchard Leigh.

Cross the stile and this road and take path LT1c opposite straight on between garden hedges, later a hedge and a fence, until you emerge into a field. Bear slightly right across this field, walking parallel to a right-hand hedge to reach a stile in another hedge ahead. Cross this and a second stile and bear slightly right, heading for the near end of a distant hedge. Here keep left of the hedge and follow it straight on. After about 250 yards, soon after the hedge bears slightly left, turn right through a gap in it (now on path CM60) and follow a left-hand hedge to reach the B4505.

Cross this road and turn left along its verge. Opposite the start of a barn at Brockhurst Farm, turn right through a hedge gap onto path CM64, then bear half right, following a fenced path to a stile. Cross this and keep straight on across a field to the corner of a hedge. Here follow a right-hand hedge, later a fence, straight on to a stile leading to Lycrome Road at Lye Green near the ´Black Cat`. Do **not** cross this stile, but turn left onto path CM63, following a right-hand hedge, crossing two wooden fences, then turning right through a hedge gap onto Lycrome Road.

Now take path CM66 along a gated concrete drive opposite. At a second set of gates, turn left through a hedge gap, then turn immediately right into a hedged path (still CM66). Follow this straight on, ignoring a right-hand stile, and, now on path AG5, eventually emerging over a stile into a field. Here keep straight on across the field to the corner of a hedge, then bear slightly right and follow a left-hand hedge, later a fence, to a stile leading to the A416.

Cross this road, bearing slightly left and take a side-road opposite. After a few yards, turn left onto the continuation of path AG5 along the drive to Pressmore Farm. Follow this drive straight on past the farm to two gates and stiles. Go straight on over the left-hand stile and follow a left-hand hedge straight on to another gate and stile. Having crossed this stile, continue to follow the left-hand hedge straight on to cross a further stile where a magnificent view opens out ahead across Chesham Vale. Now follow a fenced path downhill, passing left of a cottage, then ignoring a branching path to your left and taking path CY50 straight on downhill. On emerging through a gate onto a concrete farm road, follow it straight on downhill through Little Pressmore Farm, then continue over a stile to a road in Chesham Vale.

Turn right onto this road and follow it for a quarter mile to the 'Black Horse' (**joining the route of Herts. Walk 8**). Opposite the pub, turn right onto bridleway CY51, a hedged lane, and follow it (later becoming bridleway AG1c), winding uphill for a quarter mile, ignoring lesser branching tracks. Where the lane forks with a gate immediately ahead, turn right onto bridleway AG2 and take this sunken lane, winding uphill for a further quarter mile. Near the top of the hill, the lane turns left and continues between hedges for 300 yards to a concrete farm road near Flamstead Farm. Turn right onto this, crossing a stile by a gate to reach a barn at the farm. By the barn, turn left to reach its far end, then, **leaving Herts. Walk 8 again**, turn right onto path AG2b, passing between farm buildings and through gates and then continuing to a gate and stile. Now bear half right, passing the corner of a hedge to cross a stile onto the farm drive. Turn left onto the drive and follow it out to the A416 on the edge of Ashley Green.

Cross this road and turn left along its footway. After about 70 yards, turn right onto path AG2f between a hedge and a fence which leads you to a kissing-gate. Here bear half right across a paddock to gates, then bear half left across a second paddock to a gate onto a drive leading to a gate and kissing-gate at the end of a cul-de-sac road. Now continue straight on along this road to reach Two Dells Lane, then turn left onto it for the village hall.

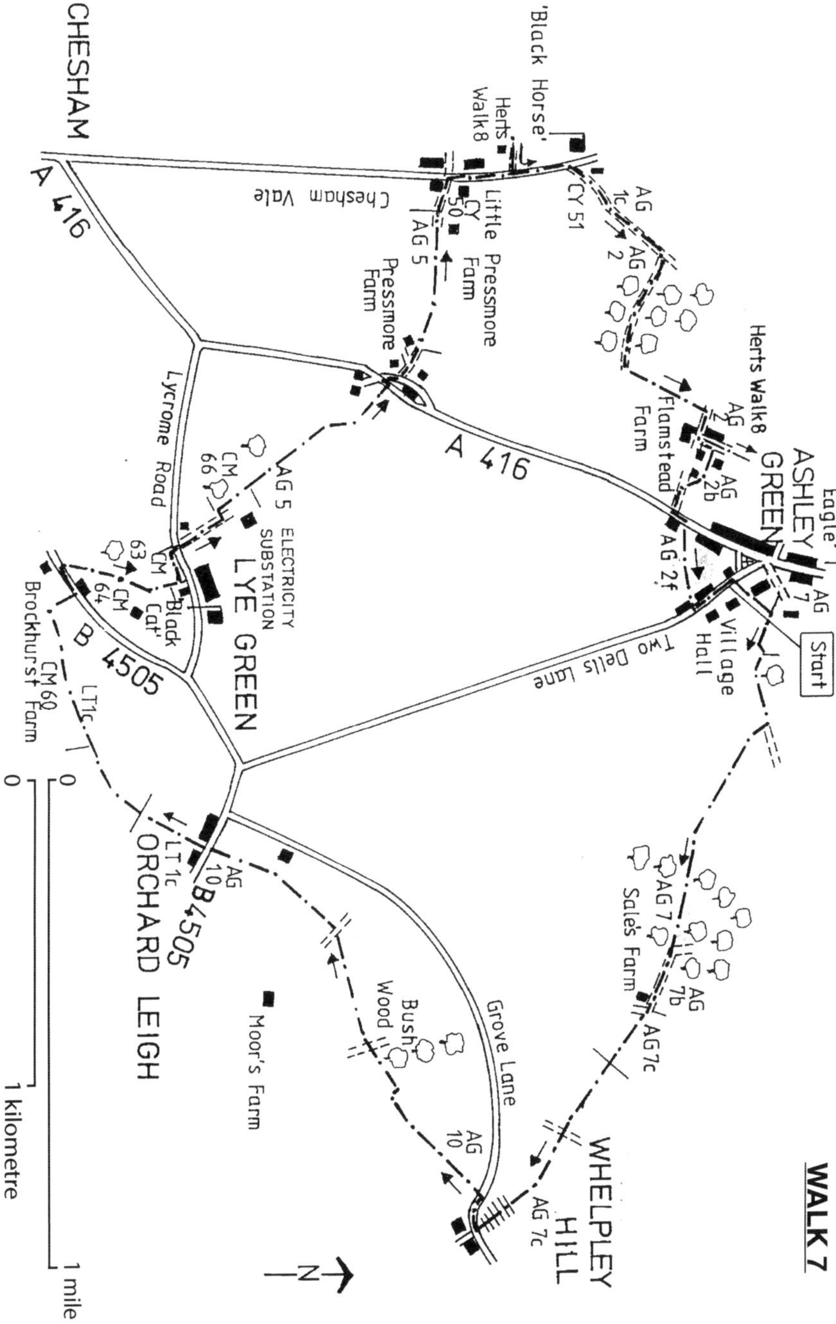

WALK 7

CHESHAM

A 416

'Black Horse'

Herts Walk 8

CheSham Vale

CY 51

Little Pressmore Farm

CY 50

AG 5

Pressmore Farm

AG 1c

AG 2

Herts Walk 8

'Golden Eagle'

Flamstead Farm

ASHLEY GREEN

AG 2a

AG 2b

AG 2f

Village Hall

AG 7

Start

A 416

Lycrome Road

CM 66

AG 5

ELECTRICITY SUBSTATION

CM 63

CM 64

'Black Cat'

LYE GREEN

Two Dells Lane

B 4505

Brockhurst Farm

CM 60

LT 1c

LT 1c

AG 10

B 4505

ORCHARD LEIGH

Moor's Farm

Bush Wood

Grove Lane

AG 10

AG 7

Sales Farm

AG 7b

AG 7c

WHELPLEY HILL

AG 7c

N→

0

0

1 kilometre

1 mile

39

WALK 8   Ley Hill

Length of Walk: 6.6 miles / 10.7 Km
Starting Point: ´The Crown`, Ley Hill.
Grid Ref: SP990019
Maps: OS Landranger Sheets 165 & 166
OS Explorer Sheet 181
Chiltern Society FP Maps Nos. 5 & 17
How to get there / Parking: Ley Hill, 2 miles east of Chesham, may be reached from the town by following the signposted route from the northern end of the town centre up White Hill, then turning right at a mini-roundabout into Botley Road and keeping straight on for 1.4 miles. At a multiple road junction near ´The Crown` and ´The Swan`, turn right and park either in a small car park on the common on the left or in the loop road in front of the pubs.
Notes: This walk may be very muddy in wet weather.

Ley Hill, though connected to Chesham by a ribbon of development along Botley Road, remains very much a typical hilltop Chiltern hamlet with its pubs and cottages scattered around its extensive common. Presumably as a result of modern motor traffic, the common, which extends to the Hertfordshire boundary, has long since ceased to be grazed by sheep and so, where it has not been converted for use as a golf course or cricket field, scrubland and even woodland have taken over.

The walk explores the hilltop plateau to the east of the village, which, being capped with clay, has traditionally been an area peppered with claypits and brickmaking activities. Despite this and its close proximity to the built-up areas of London and Watford, the plateau and the Hertfordshire villages of Flaunden and Bovingdon, through which the walk passes, retain a surprising feel of remoteness which totally belies the fact of being a mere 20 miles from Central London.

Starting with your back to ´The Crown`, cross the loop road and two further roads across the common and turn right onto path LT15, crossing the village cricket field to reach a path through the trees just right of two seats in its far corner. Now take this path through the trees, pass left of a golfing green and follow the left-hand edge of a fairway. Where the fairway forks, keep left, passing left of the 10th tee to reach a rusty gate. Here cross a road and take path LT15 straight on along the drive to Mouse Cottage. By the cottage, turn right and take path LT16 along the edge of the common to reach a road junction. Now turn left into Ashridge Lane and follow it straight on towards Latimer and Flaunden for 300 yards, ignoring a turning to the right and reaching a sharp right-hand bend. Here turn left through a bridlegate by double gates onto bridleway LT7, a track beside a right-hand fence which swings first left and then right and then continues straight on along a lofty ridge. After a third of a mile, the track begins to descend and joins a left-hand hedge. Now take a fenced, later a hedged track straight on for a further two-thirds of a mile, eventually winding its way downhill to reach a bend in the road marking the Hertfordshire county boundary in Flaunden Bottom.

Turn right onto this road and follow it for a quarter mile. Just before reaching a road junction, turn left onto fenced bridleway FD9, leading uphill into a wood called Hanging Croft. Inside the wood, keep straight on uphill to the top edge of the wood. Here ignore a branching bridleway to the right and take a fenced bridleway straight on out of the wood, heading towards a distant radio station. Now disregard a branching green lane to your right and keep straight on, swinging left and then right, until you reach a fork near the radio station. Here, **joining the reverse direction of Herts. Walk 4**, turn left onto a rough lane which leads you after nearly half a mile to the hilltop village of Flaunden.

Flaunden, locally pronounced 'Flarnden`, is an unspoilt, secluded village clustered around a crossroads of narrow lanes. Its brick-and-flint church with a bellcote, built in 1838 to replace a ruinous mediæval structure in the Chess valley one and a half miles away, is notable for being the first to be designed by the celebrated architect Sir George Gilbert Scott. It incorporates several items from its predecessor including the one-handed church clock, the ancient church bells and the fifteenth-century font allegedly once used as a nest for broody hens!

At the road junction by the church and School House, turn left, **leaving Herts. Walk 4 again**. Now, at a sharp left-hand bend, leave the road and take fenced bridleway FD1 straight on for a third of a mile to reach Long Lane in the quaintly-named Hogspit Bottom. Turn left onto this road and where the right-hand houses end, turn right onto fenced path FD16. After a quarter mile, you emerge onto another road at Venus Hill and turn left onto it, passing Venus Hill Dairy Farm, then turn right into Middle Lane. Follow it for a quarter mile, then, after rounding a sharp left-hand bend, turn right onto fenced path BV12 and follow it to Rose Farm, where the path bears right and then left between buildings to reach Water Lane. Turn right onto this road, then almost immediately left into fenced path BV13 to a kissing-gate leading to a field. Now follow a left-hand hedge to a kissing-gate at the far side of the field. Here, joining the Chiltern Way, turn left onto path BV14, following a left-hand hedge which bears left at one point. Where the hedge turns left again, bear half right across the field to the corner of another hedge, then bear slightly left with the hedge to your right and continue to a kissing-gate in the corner of the field. Go through this kissing-gate and take a fenced path straight on to a small gate. Do **not** go through this, but instead, leaving the Chiltern Way, turn left onto fenced path BV11, following a right-hand hedge. On passing through a kissing-gate into a second field, bear slightly left and take a fenced path to a road at Bovingdon Green.

Here cross the road and continue to the back of the green, then turn right and follow the back of the green past Green Farm, one end of which is timber-framed, and the cricket pavilion. On emerging at a bend in Bovingdon Green Lane, turn left onto path BV10, following a macadam drive. Where the drive forks, turn right over a stile onto path BV8 and bear half left, following a left-hand hedge to a kissing-gate. Now turn left along a path between a hedge and a fence ignoring another kissing-gate to your right. On passing through a gap in a line of trees, turn right onto a track towards the brickworks. Having passed through gates, fork left between bollards onto a fenced track past the brickworks. Near a grey building, bear slightly left, crossing another track and taking a further fenced track to reach a belt of trees at the edge of the works. Here turn right through a kissing-gate and take a fenced path which ultimately leads you out to Shantock Hall Lane (byway BV7) near a road junction at Pudds Cross.

Turn right onto this road and at the junction, cross the major road and take byway (later bridleway) BV9, a rough lane, opposite. Follow this lane, known as Pocketsdell Lane, straight on through a belt of trees for half a mile, eventually descending through a copse to a disused road. Turn left onto this, then, after 70 yards, turn left between metal posts onto another old road. Where the road turns right, leave it and take bridleway LT8, known as Green Lane, straight on along the valley bottom and county boundary for over a third of a mile until you reach the start of oak woodland on the edge of Ley Hill Common. Here bear right at a fork and follow bridleway LT8 uphill through the woodland. On reaching a crossing track, turn right onto it. Now on bridleway LT23, follow this track straight on and after a third of a mile, you return to the road junction at Ley Hill opposite 'The Crown` and 'The Swan`.

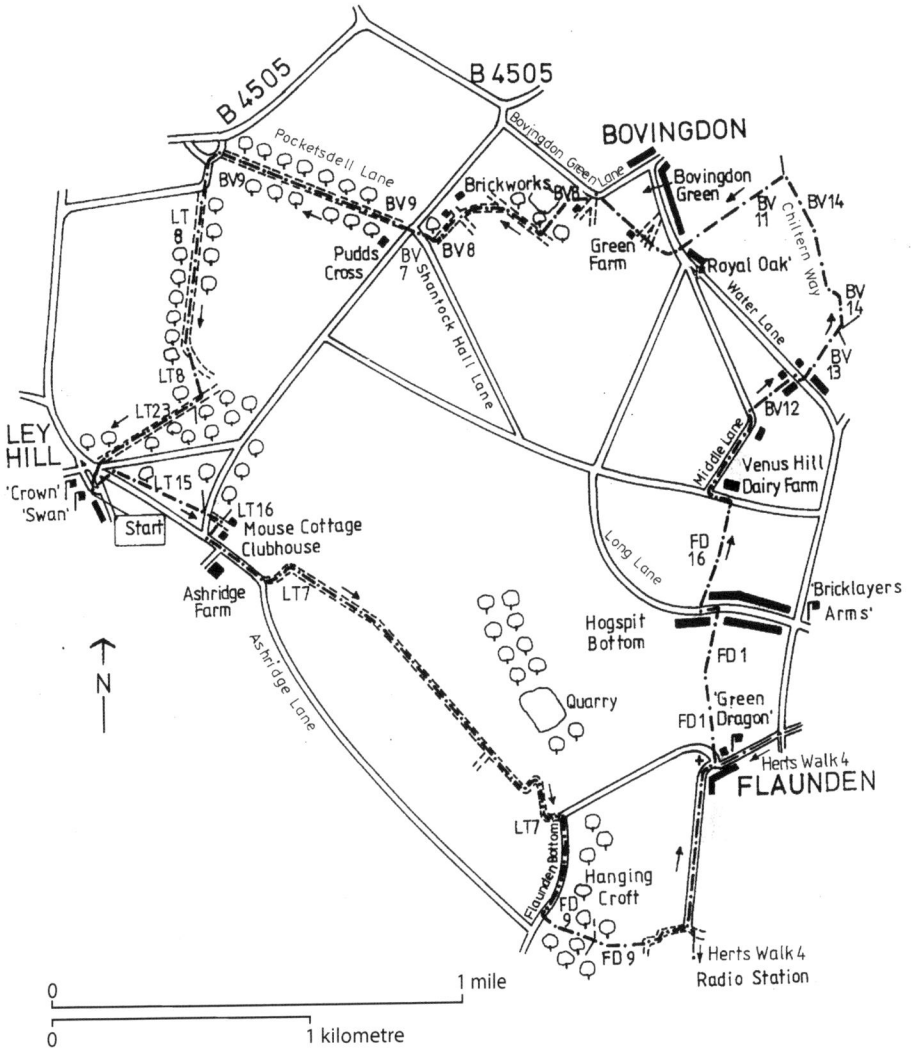

WALK 9   Chesham

Length of Walk: 7.6 miles / 12.2 Km
Starting Point: Northern end of Chesham High Street.
Grid Ref: SP961019
Maps: OS Landranger Sheet 165
OS Explorer Sheets 172 & 181 (or old Sheets 2 & 3)
Chiltern Society FP Maps Nos. 6 & 17
Parking: Car parks at Chesham Railway Station or in St. Mary's Way.
Notes: Heavy nettle growth may be encountered in places in the summer months.

Chesham, set in a deep valley at the source of the River Chess, is an industrial town which has grown considerably during the past century. Traditionally a centre of the furniture, shoe and straw-plait trades, Chesham was the birthplace of Roger Crab, the seventeenth-century eccentric believed to be the inspiration for the ´Mad Hatter` in Lewis Carroll's ´Alice in Wonderland`. The town's expansion came with the arrival of the Metropolitan Railway in 1889, which brought with it the inter-war ´Metroland` phenomenon of residential expansion in rural areas suitable for daily commuting into London. Despite this, the old part of the town around Church Street, where the source of the Chess, some quaint old cottages and the twelfth- to fourteenth-century church are situated, is well worth a visit.

The walk, which soon leaves the urban area behind, is most rewarding as it follows the northern slopes of the Chess valley to the outskirts of Latimer with fine views of this beautiful valley in places. The return over the hills to the north passes through surprisingly remote open country and culminates in a fine view of Chesham and the hills to the west before a rapid drop into the town centre.

Starting from the roundabout at the northern end of the High Street, take a road called White Hill. After about 70 yards, turn right between bollards into The Backs, soon joining a road and following it to the railway station. Where the road turns right here, take fenced macadam path CM96 straight on beside the railway. Just past the end of the station platform, turn left over a railway bridge onto path CM46, then, at the far end of the bridge, turn right. After about 40 yards, turn sharp left up a couple of steps and take a fenced terraced path which soon turns right and climbs more steeply, eventually emerging over two stiles into a field. Here go straight on across the field, aiming for the left-hand end of Dungrove Farm when it comes into view, to reach a stile. Cross this and take path CM40a straight across the next field, aiming for a tall oak tree right of the farm, to reach another stile. Do **not** cross this, but turn left onto path CM40, following a right-hand fence to a stile. Now follow the left-hand fence past the farm, crossing a further stile to reach a stile by a New Zealand (barbed-wire) gate. Cross this stile and turn right onto path CM41, following a right-hand fence to a gate and stile onto a track into the farm. Here follow a right-hand hedge straight on through two fields to reach bridleway CM34, an old green lane known as Trapp's Lane. Turn right into this lane and follow it for a quarter mile to emerge through an anti-motorcycle barrier into Rose Drive on the outskirts of Chesham.

At a crossroads ahead, turn left into Larks Rise. Where this road turns right, take path CM56 straight on between a hedge and a fence to a kissing-gate into a field. In the field, bear slightly left and follow a left-hand hedge to cross a stile in the far corner. Now turn left into Pump Lane (bridleway CM54). After a few yards, turn right over a stile onto path CM55 and bear slightly left across a field, passing left of two oaks to cross a stile at a corner of a hedge. Now follow a left-hand hedge downhill through two fields. At the bottom of the second, cross another stile and turn right into a hedged lane called Bottom Lane (bridleway CM28). At a junction of lanes, turn right and follow Bottom Lane for over a third of a mile until you emerge through a bridlegate into a field. Now bear half left onto a stony track across the field to a gate onto Latimer Road left of Milk Hall.

Turn left onto this road and at a right-hand bend, turn left into a hedged lane (bridleway CM47), then immediately turn right over a stile onto path CM27 into a field. Follow a line of trees straight across the field with the Chess not far to the right to cross two more stiles. Now bear slightly left along what is normally a worn path to a stile, then continue through a narrow paddock to a gate and stile. Having crossed the stile, take path LT22, following a right-hand garden wall and soon joining a gravel drive which bears right by a cottage to reach Blackwell Hall Lane.

Turn left onto this road and at a left-hand bend, where there is a fine view of the fifteenth-century timber-framed Blackwell Farm with its jutting upper storey to your right, take path LT5 straight on along a rough drive. Where the drive forks, keep right through a gate. At the far end of a left-hand barn, keep left at one fork and right at a second to pass through gates into a field. Here follow a right-hand hedge straight on through three fields, passing through gates at the dividing fences, to reach a small gate into Frith Wood. Now follow the edge of the wood uphill for a quarter mile. At the top of the hill, ignore a small gate to your right and bear slightly left onto a path into and through the wood. At the far side, at a fork, go straight on into the corner of a field. Here bear half right and follow the outside edge of the wood for a third of a mile, eventually with an enclosing fence to your left. On reaching a field corner, turn left and continue to a kissing-gate to your right. Now turn right through it and follow a left-hand fence to reach a stile onto a road on the outskirts of Latimer.

The village, which is to the right, has no pub, but is still worth a visit. Once known as 'Isenhampstead Latimer`, it was, for centuries, the property of the Cavendish family (later the Lords Chesham). During a prosperous period of the nineteenth century, Latimer House, the former seat of the Cavendish family, the church (designed by the celebrated architect Sir George Gilbert Scott in 1841) and much of the village were systematically rebuilt and the result is a much admired picture-book Chiltern village.

If not visiting the village, turn left along the road and follow it for a quarter mile. At the far end of a left-hand copse, at a right-hand bend, turn left through a gateway onto a track, then immediately bear half right onto path LT1 across a huge field. After just over a third of a mile, take a waymarked path into Codmore Wood just left of a kink in its edge. In the wood you soon join a track and follow it straight on through this bluebell wood, disregarding a branching path to your right. On reaching a large clearing, bear slightly left along its left-hand edge, crossing a major track and taking a grassy track straight on. Where the track ends at a crossing track, keep straight on through the trees to a stile which leads you out of the wood. Now go straight on across the field to a stile leading to Blackwell Hall Lane.

Cross this road and a stile opposite and follow a left-hand fence straight on, with White End Park with its palmhouse to your left, to reach gates and a stile into Green Lane. Cross this road and take a path opposite between a hedge and a fence. Now ignore a stile in the left-hand fence and take path LT11 straight on, soon turning right, passing a house and eventually emerging over a stile into a field. Here turn left onto path LT6, following a left-hand fence to a stile onto a drive. Cross this stile, the drive and another stile and keep straight on across two fields to a stile leading onto a rough road. Turn left onto this road (still path LT6) and after about 90 yards, turn right through a hedge gap. Now bear half left across a field to a fence gap by Cowcroft Wood. Go through this gap and bear half left onto a track into the wood. Follow this track straight on, disregarding all crossing and branching tracks and, on leaving the wood, continue past Cowcroft Farm until you reach a fork with a raised triangular island near the hamlet of Tyler's Hill.

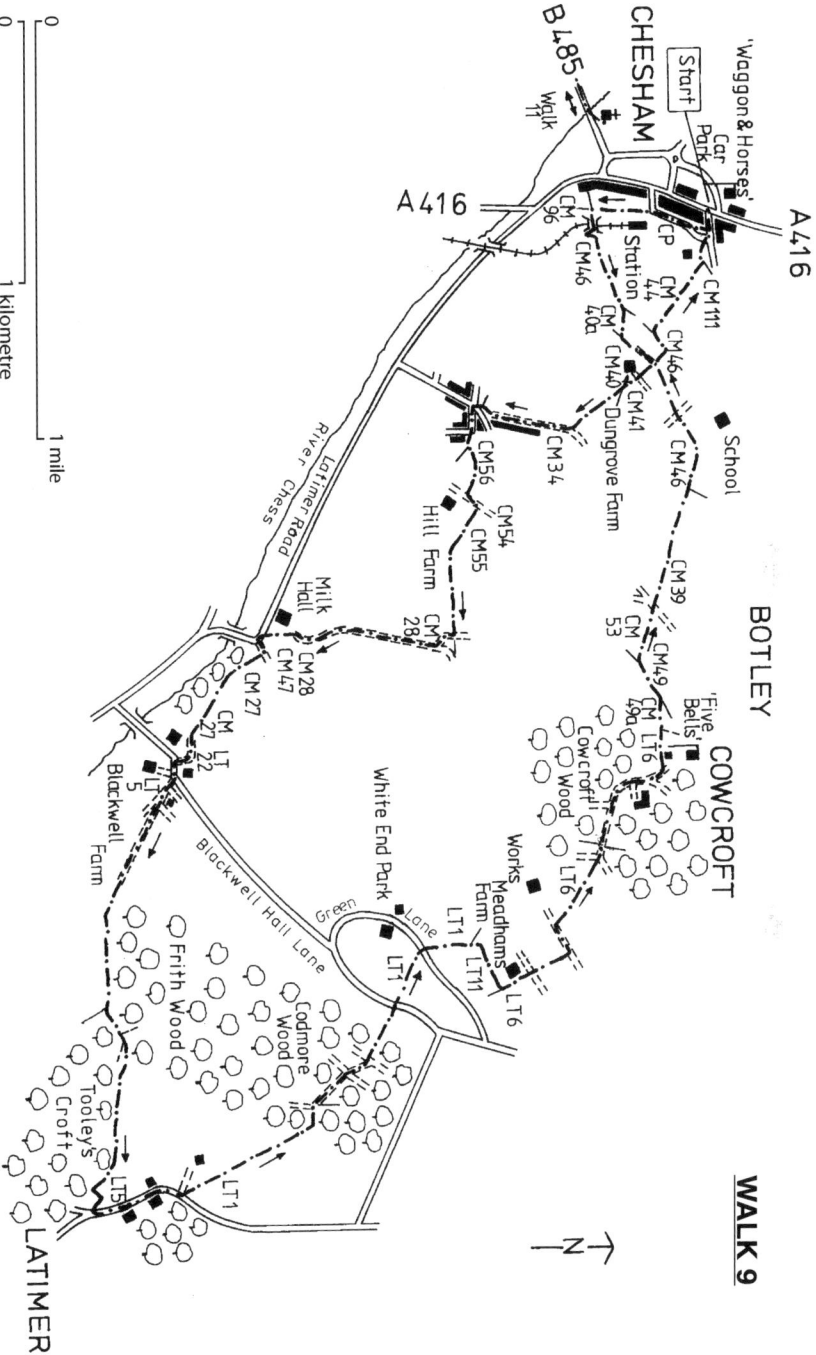

WALK 9

N→

Start

'Waggon & Horses'

CHESHAM

B485

A416

A416

Car Park

Walk

CP

Station

CM96

CM46

CM44

CM40a

CM11

CM46

CM40 Dungrove Farm

CM41

School

BOTLEY

CM34

CM56

CM54

CM55

Hill Farm

River Chess

Latimer Road

Milk Hall

CM28

CM28

CM47

CM27

CM21

LT22

LT5

Blackwell Farm

CM46

CM39

CM53

CM49

LT6

COWCROFT

'Five Bells'

'Cowcroft' Wood

LT6

Works

Meadhams Farm

LT11

LT6

LT1

White End Park

Green Lane

Lane

Frith Wood

Codmore Wood

Blackwell Hall Lane

Tooley's Croft

LT5

LT1

LATIMER

0

0

1 kilometre

1 mile

47

Here bear half left towards Tyler's Hill, then turn immediately left over a stile (still on path LT6). In the field, turn right, soon crossing another stile and following the right-hand boundary past the hamlet. Ignore a gate and stile in the right-hand fence, then cross a further stile onto path CM49 and continue to follow the fence to an old gateway. Go through this gap, then bear half left and follow a track beside a left-hand hedge. At the end of the hedge, turn right onto path CM53 along what is normally a crop break, joining a sporadic right-hand hedge and following it downhill to Bottom Lane. Having crossed this lane and a stile, take path CM39, bearing half left and following a right-hand fence uphill to cross a stile. Now bear half right across a field to a gap in the far hedge. Go through this and take path CM46, following a right-hand hedge until you reach a crossing track. Cross this track and a stile opposite and keep straight on across a field to cross a stile right of Dungrove Farm. Now bear right and take a fenced track to the far side of the left-hand field, then turn left over a stile and follow a right-hand hedge. After a further 100 yards, where the hedge bears slightly left, turn right through a waymarked hedge gap onto path CM44 and head for an oak tree ahead. Now continue straight on downhill with superb panoramic views across Chesham ahead to cross two stiles and reach macadam path CM111. Turn left onto this path and follow it, swinging right, until it joins White Hill, then keep straight on for the town centre.

WALK 10   Amersham (South)

Length of Walk: 5.7 miles / 9.1 Km
Starting Point: Broadway Car Park, Old Amersham.
Grid Ref: SU960972
Maps: OS Landranger Sheet 176 or Sheets 165 & 175
             OS Explorer Sheet 172 (or old Sheet 3)
             Chiltern Society FP Map No.6
Parking: A good car park is available on the north side of the
    Broadway in Old Amersham or on-street parking is possible
    in the High Street.

Amersham, in mediæval times a borough called ´Agmondesham`
famous for its religious dissidents and martyrs including Lollards
and later Quakers, has today one of the best-preserved traditional
High Streets of any Chiltern town. Most of its buildings date from
the sixteenth to eighteenth centuries, while several are, at least in
part, of fifteenth-century origin. The Market Hall, which protrudes
into the High Street, was built in 1682 by Sir William Drake of
nearby Shardeloes. St. Mary's Church, of thirteenth-century origin
but later extensively altered, contains numerous interesting
monuments, including many to the Drake family, and is where the
Coleshill-born poet, Edmund Waller, was christened in 1606.
Sixteenth-century Bury Farm, at the foot of Gore Hill, is also of
historical interest, as the leading Quaker, Mary Penington, took
refuge here in 1666 during her husband´s imprisonment.

 The walk traverses some fine open hill country south of the town
between Coleshill and Chalfont St. Giles and there are extensive
views, particularly in the later stages of the walk.

Starting from the entrance to the car park, take the Broadway eastwards
to the roundabout at the foot of Gore Hill (A355). Turn right onto the
A355 and follow it past Bury Farm to a roundabout on the bypass. Here
turn right onto macadam path A23, climbing to the end of a footbridge
over the bypass, then turn left onto path A23c over this bridge. At its far
end, take the path bearing slightly left to reach the back fence of gardens,
then turn right onto path A22 behind the gardens. On leaving the houses
behind, take a grassy track on the left side of a field boundary straight on
up the valley, later keeping left of a hedge. Just before an ash tree (the
first large tree along the track), turn sharp right onto path A21, entering

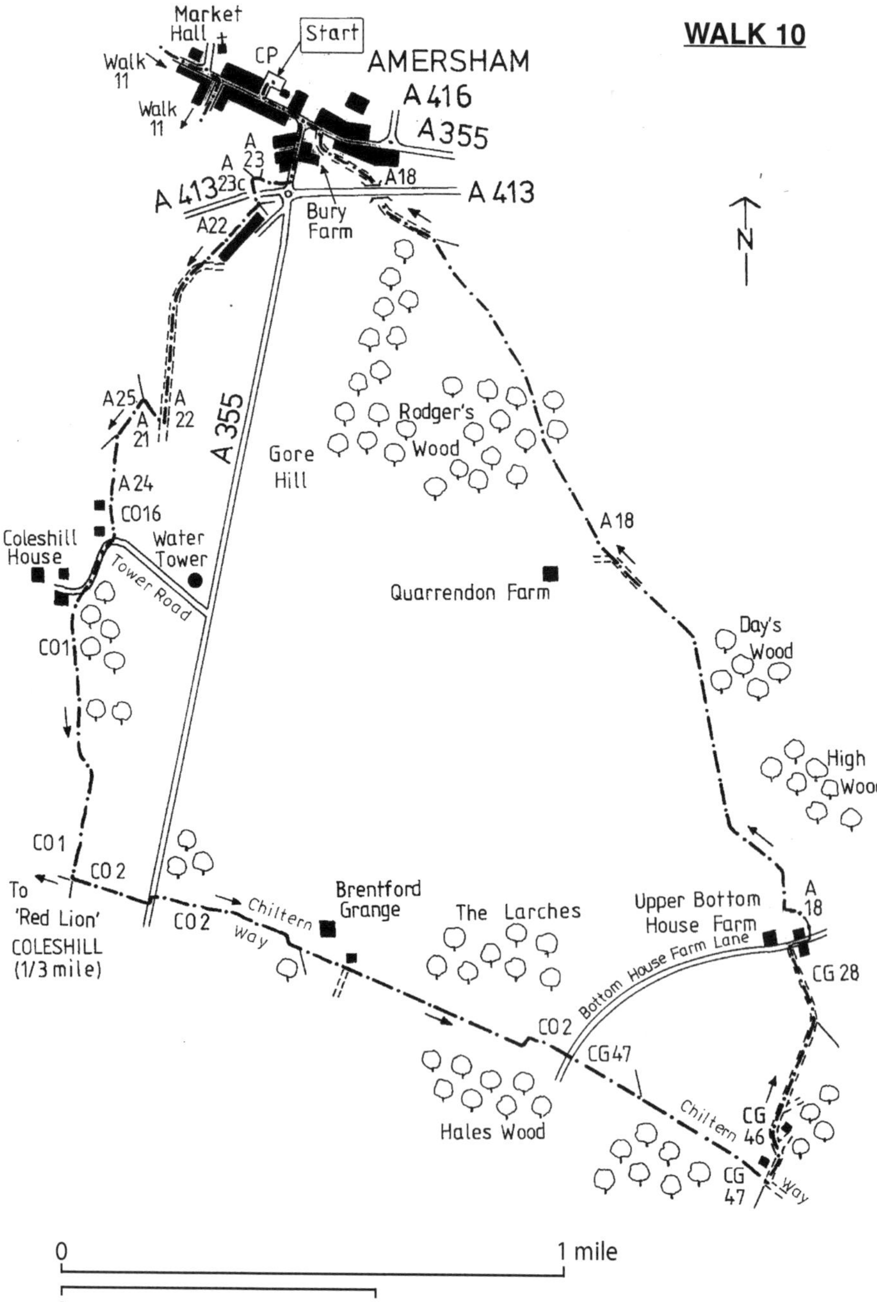

WALK 10

Market Hall

Start

Walk 11

Walk 11

CP

AMERSHAM
A 416
A 355

A 23
23c
A 413
A 22
A18
A 413
Bury Farm

N

A25
A 22
A 21
A 24
CO16
A 355
Gore Hill
Rodger's Wood
A 18

Coleshill House
Water Tower
Tower Road
Quarrendon Farm
Day's Wood

CO1

High Wood

CO 1
CO 2
Brentford Grange
The Larches
Upper Bottom House Farm
A 18

To 'Red Lion' COLESHILL (1/3 mile)
CO 2
Chiltern Way
CO 2
Bottom House Farm Lane
CG 28

CO 2
CG47
CG 46
Chiltern Way

Hales Wood
CG 47

0   1 mile

0   1 kilometre

50

the next field and heading for the right-hand end of a grass bank. Now turn sharp left onto path A25, following the bottom of the grass bank to a marker post on top of the bank. Here take path A24, bearing half left across the field to a gap left of a cottage. Now take hedged path CO16 straight on uphill to a bend in Tower Road on the edge of Coleshill.

Turn right onto the road and follow it to a sharp right-hand bend. Here take path CO1 straight on, leaving the road and crossing a stile between gates. Now follow the left-hand hedge straight on through three fields. At the far end of the third field, cross a stile, then bear half left, still following the left-hand hedge. Where the hedge turns left again, leave it and bear half right, following what is usually a crop break over a rise towards tall bushes ahead. At the far side of the field, joining the Chiltern Way, turn left onto path CO2, keeping left of a hedge and following it to the far end of the field. Here bear slightly right through a gap in the hedge, then cross a footbridge and climb some rough steps to the A355.

Cross this road, bearing slightly left to pass through a hedge gap virtually opposite. Still on path CO2, follow a right-hand hedge for a quarter mile to reach the far end of the field. Here turn right over a stile, then turn left, crossing the drive to Brentford Grange and continuing through a plantation where you ignore a branching path to your right and then cross a stile under a small oak tree. Now keep straight on across a field to a stile right of a cottage. Cross this, the cottage drive and a second stile, then follow a left-hand hedge straight on to cross another stile. Here keep straight on across the next field, joining a left-hand hedge after crossing a slight dip and following it to a hedge gap into the next field. Now follow the left-hand hedge to a stile in it, then continue on the other side of the hedge through two fields to a stile leading into the sunken Bottom House Farm Lane. On the other side of the road, climb a couple of steps to cross a stile onto path CG47, then follow what is normally a grass crop-break uphill with extensive views towards the Misbourne valley to your left to reach a redundant stile. Here go straight on, crossing two dips to reach a stile in a hedge gap right of an ash tree. Now cross this stile and keep straight on across a field to gates and a gap leading to a bend in a rough track, with a view ahead towards the Chalfonts and London.

Leaving the Chiltern Way, turn left onto this track (path CG46) and follow it, winding downhill for nearly half a mile, disregarding two branching tracks and joining path CG28, to reach Bottom House Farm Lane at Upper Bottom House Farm. Turn right onto this road, then, at the far end of the left-hand silage clamp, turn left onto path A18 along a concrete road to a flight of steps and stile leading into a field. Now follow a right-hand fence uphill to cross a stile, then, keeping right of a fence ahead, gradually diverge from it to cross a stile left of an electricity

51

pylon. Here bear half right across the next field, heading just left of the left-hand end of Day's Wood ahead and crossing a fenceline to reach a gate and stile in the far corner of the second field. (NB If there is no stile in the first fenceline, use the stile in the right-hand corner of the field). Here cross the stile and with fine views across the Misbourne valley to your right, follow the left-hand hedge for some 350 yards. Where the hedge turns left, bear slightly right across the field to the corner of a hedge, then go straight on across a further field to a stile into Rodger's Wood. Inside the wood take an obvious path to cross a stile into a field. Now bear half left across this field, heading left of a large green factory building in Amersham to reach a hedge gap. Here keep straight on across the next field to cross a stile by a gate right of the far corner, then turn left onto a track leading through an underpass under the A413 to a cattle grid, gate and stile at Bury Farm. Having crossed the stile, take a farm road, bearing right to a gate and stile onto Amersham Broadway, where a left turn returns you to your point of departure.

WALK 11   Amersham (Northwest)

Length of Walk: 10.6 miles / 17.0 Km or 10.8 miles / 17.4 Km
Starting Point: Market Hall, Old Amersham.
Grid Ref: SU958973
Maps: OS Landranger Sheet 165
OS Explorer Sheets 172 & 181 (or old Sheets 2 & 3)
Chiltern Society FP Maps Nos. 6 & 8
Parking: See Walk 10.
Notes: Heavy nettle growth may be encountered in places in the summer months.

Amersham, described in Walk 10, has owed much over the centuries to the Drake family of nearby Shardeloes, whose benefactions to the town include the seventeenth-century almshouses and the Market Hall. Shardeloes itself, which is passed early in the walk, was built for the Drake family in the classical style between 1758 and 1766 by Stiff Leadbetter and Robert Adam. The house previously on this site was where William Tothill, who is reputed to have fathered thirty-three children, entertained Elizabeth I and it was the marriage of one of his daughters to Francis Drake of Esher in about 1605 which established the Drake family at Shardeloes.

The walk, which, despite visiting the towns of Amersham and Chesham, is characterised by open and surprisingly peaceful countryside, soon leaves Amersham behind and after passing Shardeloes, explores the quiet hills around Mop End before dropping back into the Misbourne valley at the picturesque village of Little Missenden. From here, you continue over the Hyde Heath ridge into the upper reaches of the Chess valley and Chesham, then skirt Amersham-on-the-Hill on your way back to Old Amersham.

Starting from the Market Hall in the centre of Old Amersham, go eastwards along the Broadway to the second mini-roundabout, then turn right into Whielden Street (signposted to the ´Crematorium`). Just past the ´Saracens Head`, turn right into a rough lane called The Platt (path A26) and follow it past some attractive cottages and uphill to the gates of the cemetery. Here take an enclosed path right of the cemetery gates straight on to reach Cherry Lane. Cross this road and a stile opposite, then take a fenced path (still A26) along the bottom edge of a field to reach a kissing-gate. Go through this and keep straight on, soon reaching a stile onto the A413 Amersham Bypass.

Cross the stile and the bypass, then turn right along its far verge. After 25 yards, turn left over a concealed stile, then, still on path A26, bear half right and follow a right-hand hedge to reach a crossing track. Here take path A27, bearing slightly left across a large field, heading towards the chimneys of Shardeloes. At the top of a rise, the house comes into full view ahead, then go straight on, still heading for Shardeloes, to a hedge gap in the far corner of the field. Go through this, then turn left and follow a left-hand hedge, then a sporadic belt of trees and later a track along the outside edge of Wheatley Wood for half a mile. At the far end of the wood, ignore a branching track to your right and where the track turns left, go straight on, following a left-hand hedge to reach the edge of another wood called The Rough Park. Here turn right then left through a fence gap and over a stile and bear right then left, following a left-hand fence at first. Now keep straight on for a quarter mile through scrubby woodland to its far side. Here bear left, soon passing under a power-line and reaching a large pylon. Just beyond this pylon, fork right and take an obvious path along the inside edge of the wood for a quarter mile to reach Mop End Lane at the hamlet of Mop End.

Turn right onto this road, then, at a sharp right-hand bend, leave it, crossing a concealed stile right of gates ahead and taking path LM13, bearing left across a field to cross a stile at the point where a fenced track lined with young trees goes through a gap in a mature hedge. Now turn right and take a grassy track beside a right-hand hedge. At the far end of the field, go through a wide hedge gap and bear half left across the next field to a gap in the far hedge, then keep straight on across a further field to the corner of a hedge, where a rail-stile leads you into Toby's Lane. Turn right into this lane (bridleway LM26) and follow it for a third of a mile, passing through Breaches Wood. Some 200 yards beyond the wood, turn left over a stile onto path LM14 and bear half right, passing just right of a twin-trunked ash tree to reach a stile by double gates leading to a road junction on the edge of Little Missenden. Here turn right into the village and at a junction by the sixteenth-century Manor House, turn left.

The Manor House was, at one time, the home of Dr. Benjamin Bates, physician to Sir Francis Dashwood and one of the notorious ´Knights of St. Francis`, but, despite their alleged orgiastic life-style which he always denied, Dr. Bates lived to be 98! The church, next to the Manor House, is of tenth-century origin and thus one of the oldest in the Chilterns. Its chancel arch contains Roman bricks and it can also boast twelfth- to fourteenth-century murals of St. Christopher and St. Catherine, which were only rediscovered in 1931.

After passing the church, turn right over a stile by double gates onto path LM17, following the churchyard wall, then a belt of trees to cross a footbridge over the River Misbourne and reach a stile onto the A413. Cross the stile, this fast main road and a stile opposite, then keep straight on to the entrance to a fenced path between electricity poles leading to a footbridge over the Marylebone-Aylesbury railway line. At the far end of the footbridge, go straight on to a T-junction of paths, then turn left, bearing slightly right onto a well-worn path (still LM17) along the inside edge of Mantle's Wood. After a quarter mile, by Mantle's Farm to your right, ignore a crossing track and keep straight on for two-thirds of a mile, eventually leaving the wood and taking a grassy track beside a right-hand hedge to reach Hyde Heath Road at Hyde Heath.

Turn right along the roadside verge, then, at a slight left-hand bend, turn left, crossing the road and taking bridleway LM34, a stone track, after 15 yards forking right onto a woodland path. By a marker post near a cottage to your left, turn right, immediately forking left. After some 350 yards, on reaching a T-junction with a rough lane (bridleway LM33), turn left into it and follow it (soon on bridleway C2) to where it ends at white gates. Now go through a gap by these gates and take path C3 straight on along a grassy track beside a left-hand hedge, later a concrete road, for a third of a mile to reach Hawthorn Farm.

Here cross a stile by gates and turn right onto path C3a, a fenced concrete farm road. Follow this, turning right then left and continuing along a flint track beside a left-hand hedge. After passing a left-hand copse, the track turns right into White's Wood and views towards Chesham open out ahead. Here leave the track and follow the outside edge of the wood, later a right-hand hedge straight on for a quarter mile. About 100 yards short of the bottom corner of the field, turn right over a concealed stile onto path CM10, bearing half left across a field to gates and a stile in the bottom corner left of a green barn. Now cross this stile, turn right onto a macadam path beside the B485 and follow it for three-quarters of a mile into Chesham.

By the 'Queen's Head`, if wishing to look at the picturesque cottages in Church Street and visit the twelfth- to fourteenth-century church, take Church Street straight on and by no.70, cross the road and take fenced cobbled path CM2 up through a black gate to reach the church. Otherwise, turn right by the 'Queen's Head` into Wey Lane, then, after some 200 yards, turn right up Fuller's Hill. On reaching a green to your left, turn left then right into Fuller's Close. At a second T-junction, turn right again and follow a road swinging left until you reach signposted footpath CM12 through a kissing-gate to your right. Go through this gate and bear half left across a field to cross a stile by a gate. Now take path CB13, following a right-hand hedge at first, then bearing slightly left and heading for a tall chestnut tree on the skyline to reach a kissing-gate, where there are fine views over Chesham behind you. Go through this gate and keep straight on to a corner of the hedge right of the chestnut tree. Here go straight on with a hedge first to your left then to your right until you reach Mayhall Farm. Still on path CB13, keep straight on through a kissing-gate and pass between hedges to emerge into a field. Now turn right onto a track, passing between buildings, then turn left along a macadam drive to reach Copperkins Lane on the outskirts of Amersham-on-the-Hill.

Turn left along this road, then, after nearly a quarter mile, by a postbox, turn right into Weedon Lane. Just before the road bears left, turn left into a narrow hedged lane (path A41), soon crossing a road. Now keep straight on, ignoring a branching path into a wood, crossing the ends of two roads and passing Hervines Park. At the far end of the park, where the path widens into a road, turn right through a hedge gap onto path A42 and follow it along the edge of the park. At its far side, keep straight on through woodland past the end of a road to reach a railway level-crossing. Cross this and take a fenced path downhill. After a third of a mile, where the left-hand fence ends, take path A43, bearing half left across a field and heading for Coleshill Water Tower on the skyline to reach a hedge gap. Go through this, then keep straight on along the edge of a recreation ground to a hedge gap leading to a road junction. Here take Mill Lane straight on to reach the High Street, then turn left for your starting point.

WALK 11

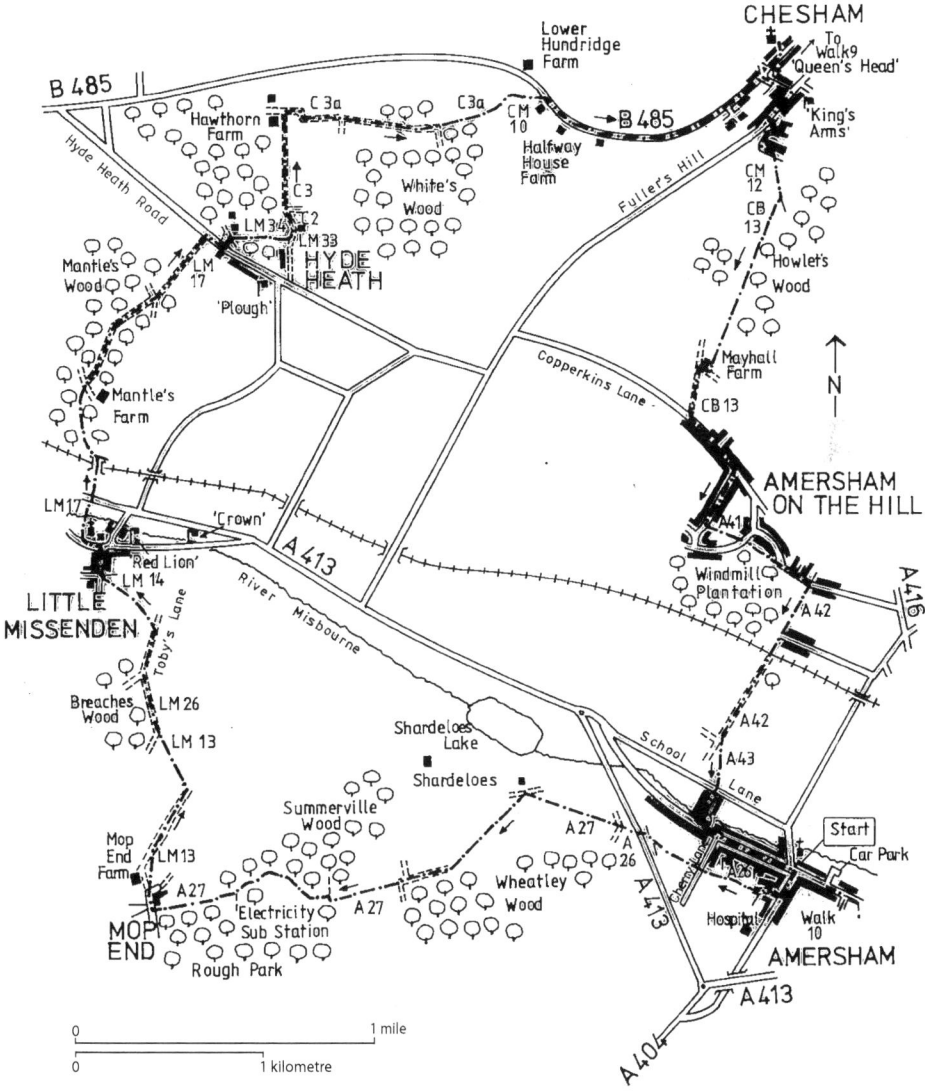

WALK 12   Great Missenden

Length of Walk: 7.3 miles / 11.8 Km
Starting Point: Entrance to Link Road car park, Great
           Missenden.
Grid Ref: SP895014
Maps: OS Landranger Sheet 165
       OS Explorer Sheet 181 (or old Sheet 2)
       Chiltern Society FP Map No.8
How to get there / Parking: Great Missenden, 4.7 miles north-
west of Amersham, may be reached from the town by taking
the A413 to the twin roundabouts at its junction with the B485
and A4128. At the second roundabout, turn left onto the
A4128, where there are car parks to your left and right.

Great Missenden, near the source of the fitful River Misbourne and
one-time home of the author, Roald Dahl, has a long, narrow,
picturesque High Street flanked by a number of old coaching inns,
cottages and small shops, some dating back to the fifteenth and
sixteenth centuries and is typical of a small town astride an old
turnpike road. Apparently there were many more coaching inns in
the past, but the arrival of the Metropolitan Railway in 1892 led to a
loss of trade. Thanks to the town's bypass, which was con-troversial
when it was built because it sliced through Abbey Park and cut the
church off from the town, it is possible to appreciate the High
Street's old world charm. The fourteenth-century church with its
Norman font, which you pass in the early part of the walk, stands on
the site of its Saxon predecessor in a prominent hillside location on
the edge of Abbey Park. The Abbey itself, founded by William de
Missenden in 1133 and in the Middle Ages, one of the largest in the
county, had to be rebuilt in the late twentieth century following a
disastrous fire which gutted the late eighteenth-century building.

     The walk soon leaves Great Missenden and the Misbourne valley
behind and explores the quiet hilltop plateau to the east separating
the Misbourne valley from the heads of some of the various Chiltern
´bottoms` which meet at Chesham to form the Chess valley, visiting
or skirting the hamlets of Hyde End, South Heath, Ballinger and
Potter Row, before descending with fine views back into the
Misbourne valley.

Starting from the entrance to Link Road car park, take Link Road (the A4128) northeastwards. On reaching the entrance to Buryfield Car Park, turn right onto path GM1e through the car park to reach the corner of a hedge. Here take a macadam path straight on beside the left-hand hedge. At the far end of the recreation ground, go straight on through a hedge gap into a residential cul-de-sac and follow it to reach a small green. Turn right along the edge of this green to a road junction at the end of the green. Now turn left onto path GM1a, a narrow road leading to the church. Take this road uphill for some 250 yards and over the bypass bridge into the churchyard. Here leave the drive and take path GM33, bearing half right across the churchyard, passing right of the church to reach a kissing-gate under a large lime tree. Go through this gate into Abbey Park, then turn left, heading for two stiles flanking a lane left of a pylon on the skyline. Cross these stiles and the lane and bear slightly right across a field over the skyline to a gate and stile. Having crossed the stile, follow a left-hand hedge, ignoring several gaps in it and eventually reaching a stile in a corner of the field. Cross this and follow a right-hand hedge through two fields. In the second field, look out for a stile in the right-hand hedge. On reaching it, cross it and take a path through a copse to Hyde Lane.

Turn right onto this road and follow it past Chapel Farm. Before reaching Hyde Farm, turn left onto path GM27, a concrete farm road, going straight on past the farm and descending into the valley bottom. Where the concrete road turns right just before its surface ends, leave it, crossing a stile by a gate and keep straight on, passing left of a copse concealing an old gravel pit, to cross a stile on path GM26 into the end of a tree belt. Now take a path straight on through the tree belt, which, in late April, is profuse with bluebells, to reach Hyde Heath Road. Turn left onto this road and at its junction with the B485 at Hyde End, turn right then almost immediately left, crossing the main road and taking path GM21, a macadam private road. Where this road turns left into Middlegrove Farm, bear slightly right, leaving the road and passing through trees. On leaving the wood, bear slightly left going through gates between farm buildings. Now keep straight on through a yard, then bear slightly left through a belt of young trees to a stile. Here bear half left across a field to cross a stile in the far corner, then follow a left-hand hedge climbing gently. Just before reaching the far end of the field, turn left through a hedge gap into a fenced path and follow it to a stile leading to a gravel lane called Wood Lane at South Heath.

Take this lane straight on to where it becomes a macadam road, then, about 30 yards further on, turn right through a gap by a gate into a gravel lane leading into Redding Wick Wood. On entering the wood, ignore a branching path to the right, then keep left at a fork and continue straight on along the inside edge of the wood for some 200 yards until you reach a crossing path. Here turn right onto path GM19 and after a few yards, where this forks, take the left-hand option straight on, passing just left of moated earthworks (which the name of the wood suggests to be the site of a lost village) and keeping straight on across the wood to cross a stile at the far corner. Now follow a right-hand hedge straight on to a gate. Do **not** go through the gate, but, instead, turn left over a stile and take a fenced path to cross another stile. Now follow the right-hand hedge straight on to cross a third stile, then turn right and continue to follow the hedge, wiggling to the left at one point. Where it turns right again, follow it again to reach the drive to Redding's Farm. Turn left onto this drive and follow it (later on path C4c) to reach Little Hundridge Lane.

Turn left onto this road, then, almost immediately, turn right onto path C5 through an unusual stile into a wood called Black Grove. Now bear half left and follow a path descending to reach fenced bridleway C4b in a valley bottom known as Herbert's Hole. Turn left onto this bridleway and follow it to a road junction by a cottage. Here go straight on past the cottage, then, by the far end of its garden, turn right over a stile by a gate onto path GM18a, taking a fenced path uphill, ignoring a stile into a wood. At the top corner of the left-hand field, cross a stile and take enclosed path C59 to reach a bend in bridleway C58. Take this straight on, then, at a sharp right-hand bend, turn left through a kissing-gate by a gate onto path GM18. Just past a pond, turn right through a small gate and take a fenced path through two fields. At the far side of the second field, go through a kissing-gate and turn left onto path GM7a, following a left-hand hedge with views over Ballinger Bottom to your right to reach a gate and kissing-gate into a wood. Go through the kissing-gate and take a path straight on along the top edge of the wood. Where this path eventually bears right and descends, turn left and take a fenced path to a duck-under rail leading to Chiltern Road in Ballinger.

Turn right onto this road and at a road junction, turn right again, then almost immediately turn left through a gate onto path GM7 and take a grass path straight on through some allotments to a small gate into the end of Blackthorne Lane. Go through this gate, then turn right through a hedge gap and turn left to follow a left-hand hedge to a stile into Hawthorn Wood. Cross this stile and take waymarked path L29 straight on for some 300 yards, ignoring a crossing track and a path merging from your right and passing a plantation. At the far end of the plantation, turn right, following the waymarked path to cross a stile into a field. Bear slightly right across the field to the right-hand end of a hedge ahead, then go past it and turn left, following a left-hand hedge and later the garden fence of a much-extended cottage. Just past the cottage, join its drive and follow it straight on into a lane. At a junction of lanes by some cottages, turn left and take a flinty lane (bridleway L42) uphill, bearing right and then left to reach a gate and stile just beyond a seat. Cross the stile and

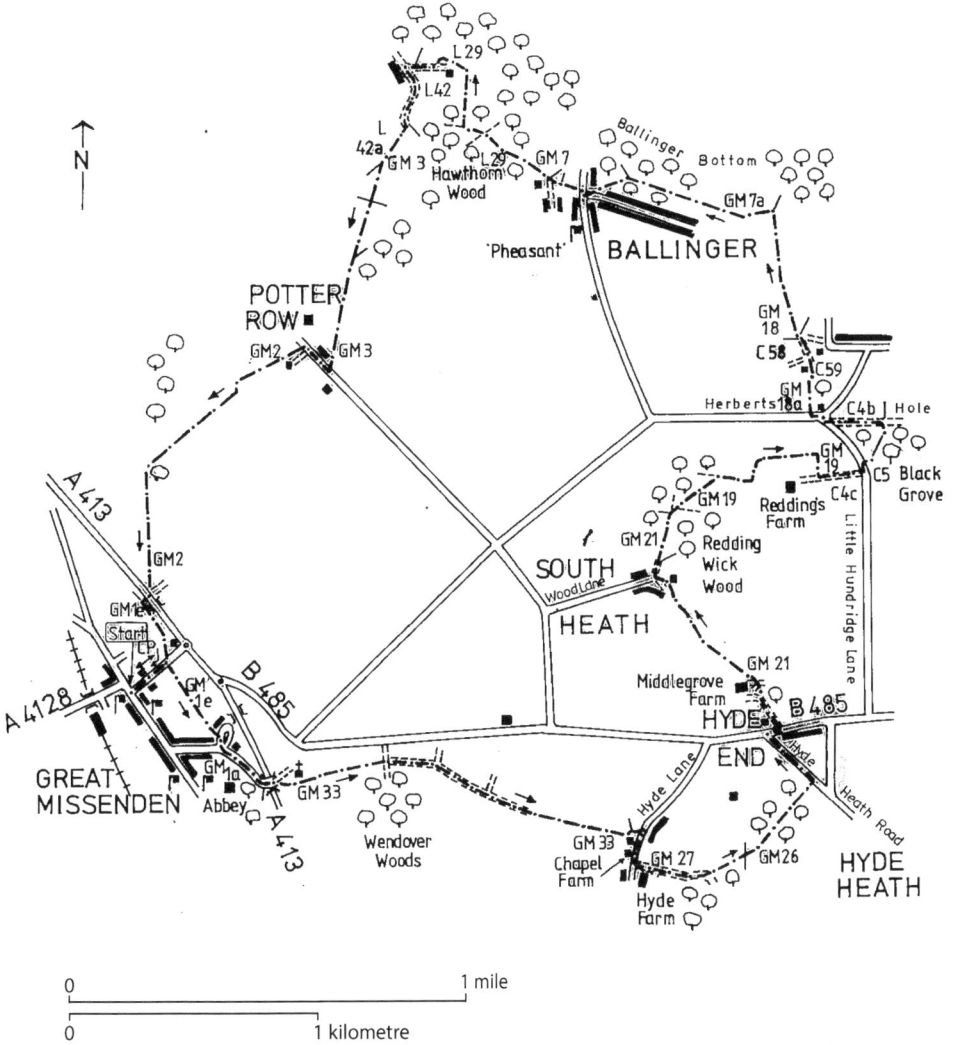

WALK 12

THE LEE

N

L29
L42
L42a
L
GM3
Hawthorn
Wood
L29
GM7
Ballinger Bottom
GM7a
'Pheasant'
BALLINGER

POTTER ROW
GM2
GM3
GM
18
C58
C59
GM
Herberts18a
C4b Hole
GM
19
C5 Black Grove
C4c
A413
GM2
GM19
Reddings Farm
GM21
Redding Wick Wood
SOUTH
Wood Lane
HEATH
GM2
GM1e
Start
CP
B485
Middlegrove Farm
GM 21
HYDE
END
B485
Little Hundridge Lane
A4128
GREAT MISSENDEN
GM1e
GM1a
Abbey
GM33
A413
Wendover Woods
GM33
Chapel Farm
Hyde Farm
GM 27
GM26
Hyde Lane
Heath Road
HYDE HEATH

0   1 mile
0   1 kilometre

61

turn left and take a flinty lane (bridleway L42) uphill, bearing right and then left to reach a gate and stile just beyond a seat. Cross the stile and take path L42a following a right-hand hedge. Where the hedge turns right, leave it and take path GM3 straight on to cross a stile by a pylon where three hedges meet. Now go diagonally across a field past another pylon to a stile. Having crossed this, go diagonally across another field to cross two further stiles, then keep straight on, crossing a further field diagonally, passing the corner of a hedge to reach a gap between a gate and a redundant stile by a tall oak tree left of a long cottage, which leads to the road at Potter Row.

Turn right onto this road, following it past several cottages, then, by the entrance to ´Silver Birches`, turn left over a stile onto path GM2. Now follow a left-hand hedge to cross a stile by a gate, then continue to follow the left-hand hedge to a stile in it. Turn left over this and cross a narrow field, then turn right and follow a left-hand hedge to the far end of the field. Here go through a gap and bear slightly left across the next field, with a view of Great Missenden Church to your left, to cross two stiles. Now keep straight on, joining a left-hand hedge by an ash tree and following it downhill to cross a stile in the bottom corner of the field. Here bear half left across a field to a stile, then cross two further fields diagonally, heading for a large green road sign on the A413. By this sign, turn right over a stile by a gate to reach the A413, cross this road carefully and climb a stile by a gate. Now turn left onto path GM1e to cross a stile by a gate, then follow a right-hand hedge through two fields to a gate and kissing-gate leading to the A4128, where you turn right for your starting point.

WALK 13   Great Kingshill

Length of Walk: 5.6 miles / 9.0 Km
Starting Point: Great Kingshill sports pavilion.
Grid Ref: SU878981
Maps: OS Landranger Sheet 165
       OS Explorer Sheet 172 (or old Sheet 3)
       Chiltern Society FP Map No.12
How to get there / Parking: Great Kingshill, 3.2 miles north of
       High Wycombe, may be reached from the town centre by
       taking the A4128 northwards towards Great Missenden for
       3.5 miles. In the village, by the ´Red Lion`, turn right into
       The Common where there is a car park on the left.

Great Kingshill, the name of which derives from the manor having been held by the Crown in Norman times, was, 150 years ago, little more than a few scattered cottages around a vast upland common. Following inclosure, however, when the common was reduced to its present size, this hamlet started to grow to become the relatively large village we know today and it is for this reason that most of its buildings are of Victorian or more recent origin. Like its neighbour Prestwood, Great Kingshill was, at one time, noted for its abundant cherry orchards necessary for making the Buckinghamshire speciality of cherry pie, but today most of the orchards have, unfortunately, given way to the incessant pressure for ´in-filling` development.

The walk soon leaves this outpost of suburbia behind and explores the beautiful landscape of steep-sided ridges and bottoms interspersed with Chiltern beechwoods to be found at the head of the Hughenden valley, before climbing to skirt Prestwood on its way back to Great Kingshill.

Starting from Great Kingshill sports pavilion on the edge of the green in Common Road, take the road southwards for about 80 yards, then turn right through a squeeze-stile onto path H58, following a left-hand hedge across the recreation ground to a hedge gap leading to the A4128. Cross the main road and take New Road straight on. At the far end of New Road, turn left onto fenced path H60 and follow it to Pipers Lane. Turn right onto this road and follow it for a quarter mile to the gates of Pipers Corner School. Here, joining the reverse direction of **Walk 19**, turn right

WALK 13

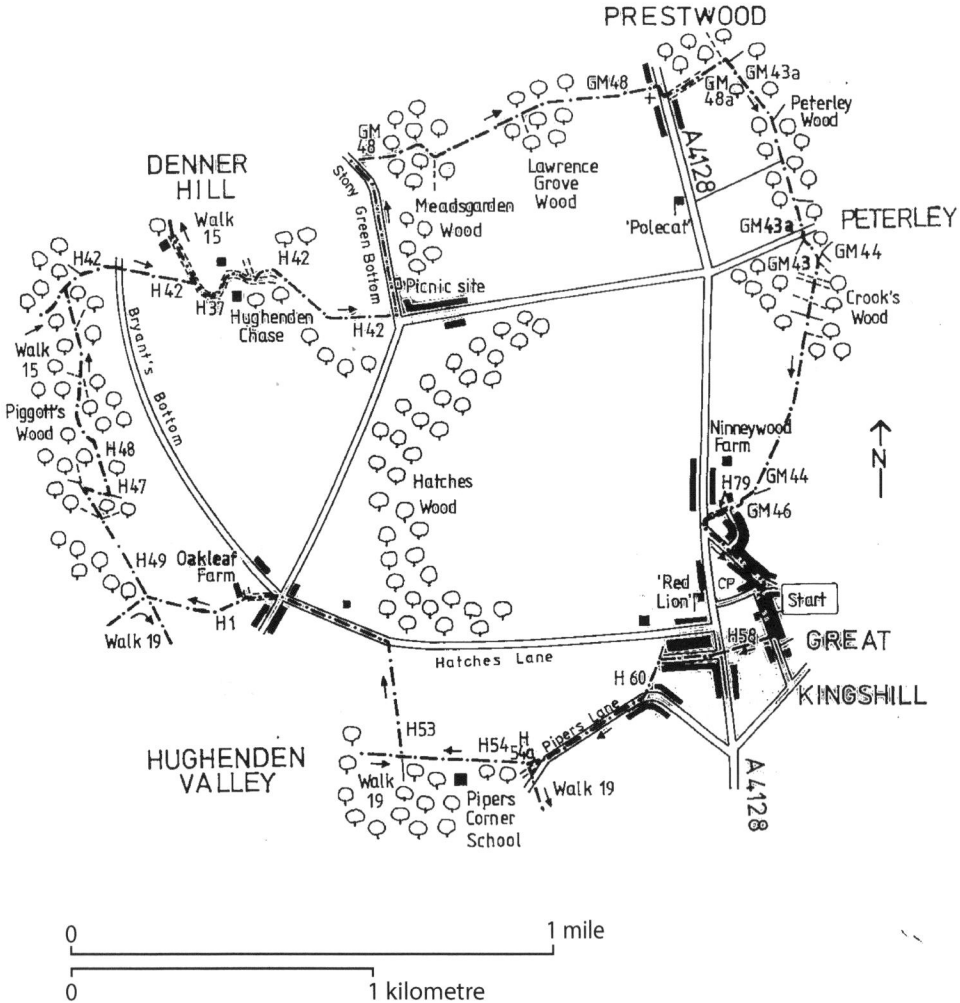

PRESTWOOD

GM43a

Peterley Wood

GM48

GM 48a

A4128

DENNER HILL

Lawrence Grove Wood

Meadsgarden Wood

'Polecat'

GM43a

PETERLEY

GM44

GM43

Stony Green Bottom

Walk 15

H42

H42

H42

H37

Hughenden Chase

Picnic site

H42

GM43

Crook's Wood

Walk 15

Bryant's Bottom

Piggott's Wood

H48

H47

Hatches Wood

Ninneywood Farm

H79

GM44

GM46

N

H49 Oakleaf Farm

H1

Walk 19

'Red Lion'

CP

Start

Hatches Lane

H58

GREAT KINGSHILL

H 60

Pipers Lane

HUGHENDEN VALLEY

H53

H54

H

Walk 19

A4128

Walk 19

Pipers Corner School

| 0 | 1 mile |

| 0 | 1 kilometre |

64

through a kissing-gate by a gate onto path H54, then immediately turn left and follow a left-hand hedge to pass through two kissing-gates. Now take a fenced path along the edge of woodland to a kissing-gate in the right-hand fence. Leaving **Walk 19**, turn right through this kissing-gate onto path H53, going straight across a field with a fine view ahead of the three ´bottoms` which converge to form the Hughenden valley, aiming for the left-hand end of Hatches Wood to reach a kissing-gate. Now keep straight on downhill to a kissing-gate into Hatches Lane. Turn left and follow this road downhill for a quarter mile to a crossroads.

Here cross the major road and take path H1 straight on up the drive to Oakleaf Farm. Where the drive bears right and its macadam surface ends, keep left, taking a fenced path left of a bungalow straight on to cross a stile. Now keep straight on over a rise to a concealed kissing-gate, then bear half right across the corner of the next field to a hedge gap and concealed stile (where you again meet, but do not join the route of **Walk 19**). Here go through the kissing-gate and take path H49 straight on uphill, passing just right of a copse and a pair of Scots pine trees to reach a stile into Piggott's Wood. Inside the wood, disregard a path to the right. Now take a waymarked path veering left, then right, then left again. After 120 yards, turn right onto path H47, then, after a further 80 yards, turn left at a crossways onto path H48 and follow this path along the contours of the hill, ignoring all branching or crossing paths or tracks. After a third of a mile, disregard a path forking downhill to your right and go straight on until you reach a waymarked T-junction with path H42. Joining **Walk 15**, turn right onto this path and follow it downhill to cross a stile by a gate out of the wood. Now follow a left-hand hedge straight on to a stile and gate onto a road in Bryant's Bottom.

Having crossed this stile and road and a stile by a gate opposite, bear half right up a steep bank to a gate and stile by the corner of a garden hedge. Cross the stile and bear half right to a stile leading to a macadam drive (bridleway H37). Cross the stile and turn right onto this drive, leaving **Walk 15** again. Now follow the drive through white gates, then swinging left then right around a large white house now known as ´Hughenden Chase`. Having passed the house, where a drive merges from the left, turn left over a stile onto the continuation of path H42, then turn right and follow a right-hand fence and tree belt, swinging right to reach another stile. Cross this and follow a right-hand hedge downhill to a stile onto Hampden Road near a road junction in Stony Green Bottom.

Turn left onto this road and follow it for a third of a mile, passing a picnic site. On reaching a left-hand bend, pass a junction of right-hand hedges, then, some 40 yards further on, turn right through a kissing-gate by a gate onto path GM48 and bear half right across a field to cross a stile into Meadsgarden Wood in a corner. In the wood, follow a left-hand fence straight on uphill. Near the top of the hill, follow the path leaving the fence and bearing right to reach a kissing-gate. Now take a fenced path between fields straight on to a kissing-gate into Lawrence Grove Wood. Here take a woodland path straight on to reach a kissing-gate into another field. Now keep straight on, following a left-hand hedge across a dip to another kissing-gate, then take a path between hedges straight on to a kissing-gate onto the A4128 on the edge of Prestwood.

Here turn right, passing Prestwood's Victorian church. Opposite a flint cottage, turn left onto path GM48a, a rough lane along the edge of a wood which narrows into a fenced path. At the far side of the right-hand field, turn right onto a crossing path into Peterley Wood, then immediately fork right onto bridleway GM43a. Now follow this obvious woodland bridleway straight on for over a third of a mile, ignoring a branching track to your left, then keeping right at a fork, disregarding a branching path to your right and eventually reaching a road at Peterley.

Cross this road and take path GM43 through a kissing-gate virtually opposite. Now follow this winding path for about 80 yards to a waymarked crossways. Here turn right onto path GM44 and follow its winding course, disregarding crossing tracks and paths and soon entering and traversing a belt of mature woodland. At the far side of this woodland, take a fenced path straight on to reach a stile. Cross this and go past a pond, then bear slightly left across a field to a stile in the far corner. Having crossed this, take fenced path GM46, crossing another stile, then enclosed path H79, soon crossing the end of a residential cul-de-sac and continuing along a bollarded lane to the A4128 on the edge of Great Kingshill. Turn left onto this road, then, at a road junction, turn left into Stag Lane and follow this road for some 250 yards. Now take the first turning right, The Common, which leads you back to your point of departure.

WALK 14   Little Hampden

Length of Walk: 6.4 miles / 10.3 Km
Starting Point: Car park at Little Hampden.
Grid Ref: SP858040
Maps: OS Landranger Sheet 165
       OS Explorer Sheet 181 (or old Sheet 2)
       Chiltern Society FP Maps Nos. 3 & 12
How to get there / Parking: Little Hampden, 2.6 miles north-west of Great Missenden, may be reached from the town by taking the Princes Risborough and Ellesborough road westwards for 2 miles, then turning right into a lane signposted to Little Hampden. A car park is available on common land on the right at the end of the road.

Little Hampden, on a high ridge at the end of a long winding cul-de-sac lane, has often, with justification, been described as the remotest village in the Buckinghamshire Chilterns. For all this, an extensive network of inviting footpaths radiates from it. This tiny village with a small thirteenth-century church containing thirteenth- and fifteenth-century murals, its picturesque old, but extended, village pub and few farms and cottages, was prior to 1885, a separate parish. Today, however, it is grouped together with Great Hampden on the opposite side of Hampden Bottom and it is principally this enlarged and particularly scenic parish which the walk explores, passing Hampden House and Great Hampden Church.

Starting from the end of the public road and far end of the car park at Little Hampden, turn right onto path G50, the right-hand of two paths into woodland on Little Hampden Common, following an obvious path downhill. In the valley bottom, keep left, following the winding path to reach a track at the edge of the wood. Do **not** join this track, but bear half left through a hedge gap and follow the right-hand hedge downhill to a corner of Hampdenleaf Wood. Here join a track, entering the wood, then immediately fork right. At a second fork, by the corner of a field to your right, keep left, taking a waymarked track steeply uphill. Soon the track bears right, climbing more gently to a path junction at the edge of a more mature plantation. Here turn right onto path G47, taking a waymarked track along the edge of this plantation and then through a young plantation for over a quarter mile to reach crossing path G49.

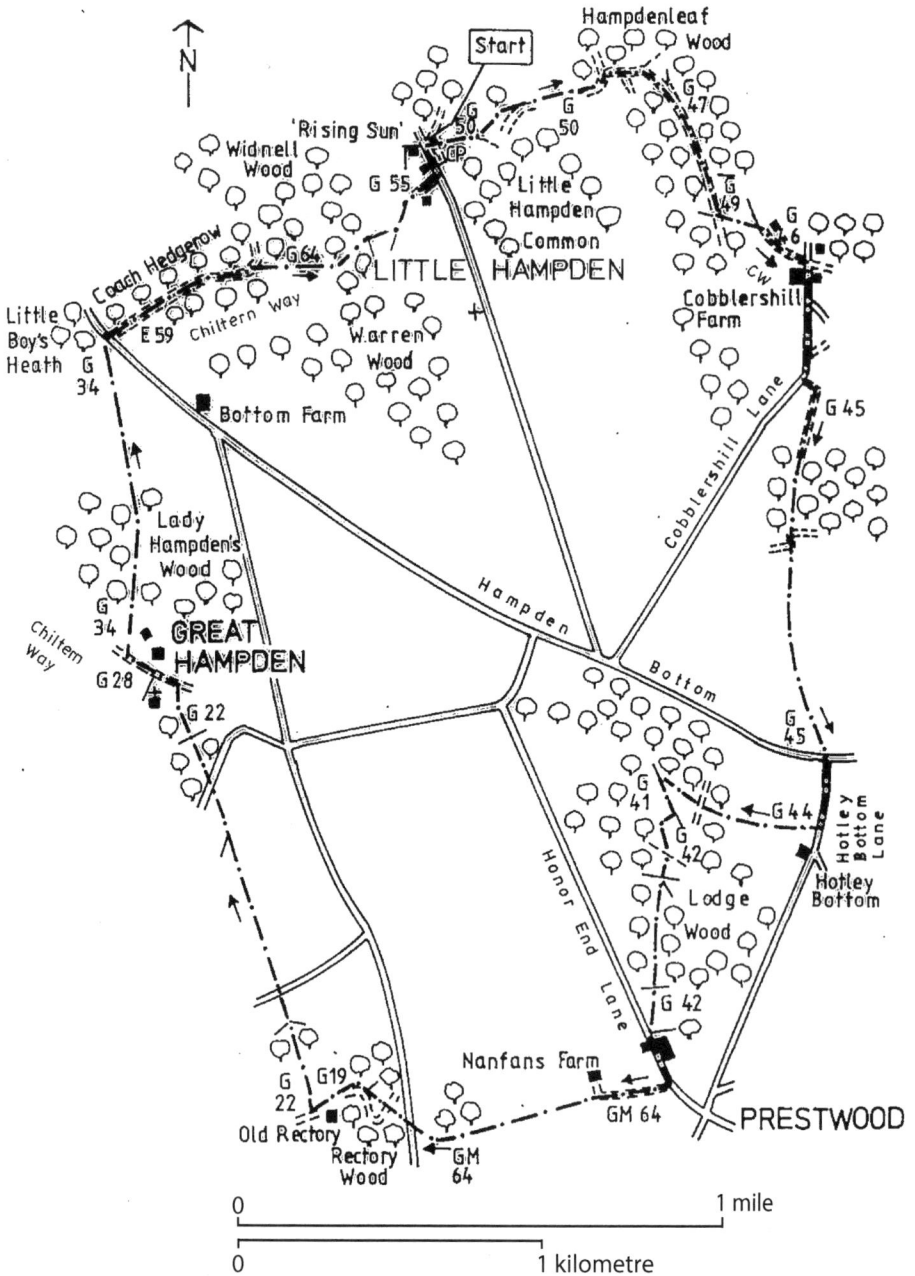

Joining the Chiltern Way, turn left onto this path, soon crossing a stile into a field. Bear half right across this field to cross two stiles left of an electricity pole, then take bridleway G46, bearing slightly right and following a rough lane to Cobblershill Lane at Cobblers Hill.

Leaving the Chiltern Way, turn right onto this road for a quarter mile, ignoring a side-turning and a grassy track to the left. Just after a right-hand bend at the far side of a copse, turn left through a gate onto path G45, a short green lane. On emerging into a field, follow the track, turning right alongside a right-hand hedge to reach a gap in the corner of the field. Go straight on through this and take a defined path along the inside edge of a wood until you join a track and emerge into a field. Where the track turns right, leave it and follow the right-hand hedge straight on downhill to a hedge gap in the bottom corner of the field. Go through this and bear half left across the next field to a hedge gap at a road junction in Hampden Bottom.

Cross the major road and take Hotley Bottom Lane opposite uphill for some 250 yards, then turn right onto path G44 up some steps and through a hedge gap into a fenced path. Now continue uphill past a garden into a field, then follow the right-hand hedge straight on to enter Pepperboxes Wood. In the wood, take a defined path straight on, ignoring a crossing track and passing through a mature coniferous plantation. At a T-junction, turn left onto path G41, climbing to a woodland crossways by a seat. Here turn right onto path G42, soon bearing left. Now take this path straight on through Lodge Wood, ignoring all crossing and branching paths until, after nearly half a mile, you reach a gate and stile leading to Honor End Lane on the outskirts of Prestwood.

Turn left onto this road and after about 150 yards, turn right onto path GM64 along the drive to Nanfans Farm. Where the drive turns right into the farm, leave it and go straight on through a kissing-gate, then follow a right-hand fence to a kissing-gate into a field. Bear slightly right across the field to a kissing-gate in a dip, then continue uphill to join a left-hand fence and follow it to a stile. Cross this, then bear slightly right across a field to the corner of a copse. Keeping left of the copse, follow its edge downhill. At its bottom corner, bear half right across the field to a flight of steps leading down to a road.

Turn right onto this road, then almost immediately left onto path G21 uphill through Rectory Wood. On reaching a macadam drive, turn left and follow it, soon bearing sharp right and then continuing uphill to a left-hand bend. Where a gate comes into view ahead, leave the drive and go to the gate. Now on bridleway G19, do not go through it, but instead turn left and follow a right-hand fence to the far end of the field. Here bear half left through a hedge gap and by a hollybush, turn right over a concealed rail-stile onto path G22. Go straight on through the trees, then continue along a fenced path at the side of a field to a stile at the corner of the hedge. Now keep straight on across a large field to a hedge gap right of an electricity pylon. Go through this, cross a road and go through a hedge gap opposite, then keep straight on across the next field to the corner of a hedge. Here follow a left-hand hedge straight on to cross a stile, then bear slightly right and follow an avenue of trees, recently replenished by the planting of numerous saplings, to a stile onto another road. Cross this road and still on path G22, go through a kissing-gate opposite, then bear half right and follow the continuation of the avenue to another kissing-gate onto a macadam drive by Great Hampden Church.

Built in the thirteenth century, Great Hampden Church contains various monuments to the Hampden family, including its most famous member, John Hampden, cousin of Oliver Cromwell, whose refusal to pay King Charles I's unjust ship tax in 1635 was one of the events leading to the Civil War. Wounded at the Battle of Chalgrove Field in 1643, John Hampden died soon after in Thame and was buried at Great Hampden, but his grave is unmarked. Nearby battlemented Hampden House, the seat of the Hampden family and their descendants, the Earls of Buckinghamshire, from before the Norman conquest till the Second World War, was partially built in the fourteenth century, considerably extended by John Hampden and much altered again in 1750 with ceilings and fireplaces by Adam.

Turn left onto the drive (bridleway G28) and follow it past the church and house and through gates. Now, rejoining the Chiltern Way, turn right over a stile by gates onto path G34, bearing slightly left across a field to a stile into Lady Hampden's Wood. Here take a wide fenced path downhill through the wood to a gate and stile where fine views open out across Hampden Bottom, home of the late actor and country-lover Sir Bernard Miles. Now go straight on to the far corner of the field where two tree belts meet. Here cross a stile by gates, a road and a stile by gates opposite into a tree belt called Coach Hedgerow, noted for its bluebells, and take path E59 along a timber track gently uphill through the tree belt. At the far end of the tree belt, where the track bears left into Widnell Wood, turn right onto a crossing track, leaving the wood. Now take path G64, bearing slightly right across the field passing through one gate and reaching a second in the top hedge, then go straight on uphill through a plantation. On emerging into a field, leaving the Chiltern Way, go straight on, then, just past the far end of mature woodland to your right, bear half left onto path G55 to reach another hedge gap. Go through this and continue between a hedge and a fence, then along a concrete drive, to the road at Little Hampden almost opposite the car park.

WALK 15   Hampden Row

Length of Walk: 5.5 miles / 8.8 Km
Starting Point: ´Hampden Arms`, Hampden Row.
Grid Ref: SP845015
Maps: OS Landranger Sheet 165
             OS Explorer Sheets 172 & 181 (or old Sheets 2 & 3)
             Chiltern Society FP Map No.12
How to get there / Parking: Hampden Row, 5.4 miles northwest
    of High Wycombe, may be reached from the town by taking
    the A4128 northwards for two miles and leaving it at a
    roundabout where it turns right. Now go straight on up the
    Hughenden valley for a further three-quarters of a mile. By
    the ´Harrow`, turn right and after half a mile, turn left,
    following signposts to Bryant's Bottom. Take this road
    through Bryant's Bottom for 2.3 miles to a crossroads. Here
    turn right towards Hampden and Great Missenden and turn
    right again at a T-junction. At a road junction by the
    ´Hampden Arms`, turn right and seek a suitable place to
    park.

Hampden Row, the village attached to the Great Hampden Estate, is
typical of many such villages attached to major country estates in
being some distance from its church and manor house on the edge of
the parish common. Its name is, indeed, apt, as it consists largely of
a pub and row of cottages along one side of a road with the common
on the other which includes a particularly attractive cricket field laid
out by the last Earl of Buckinghamshire in 1950. The village derives
its   name   from   the   Hampden   family   (later   the   Earls   of
Buckinghamshire), who have held the manor since before the
Norman conquest and whose most famous member was John
Hampden (1594 - 1643), the leading Parliamentarian politician and
soldier, whose refusal to pay King Charles I's ship tax in 1635 was
one of the events leading to the Civil War. Wounded at the Battle of
Chalgrove Field in 1643, he died soon after in Thame and was
buried at Great Hampden, but his grave is unmarked.
     The walk explores the heavily-wooded country of steep ridges and
deep bottoms, so characteristic of Chiltern backland, visiting the
village of Speen and the hamlets of Turnip End, Flowers Bottom,
Upper North Dean and Denner Hill.

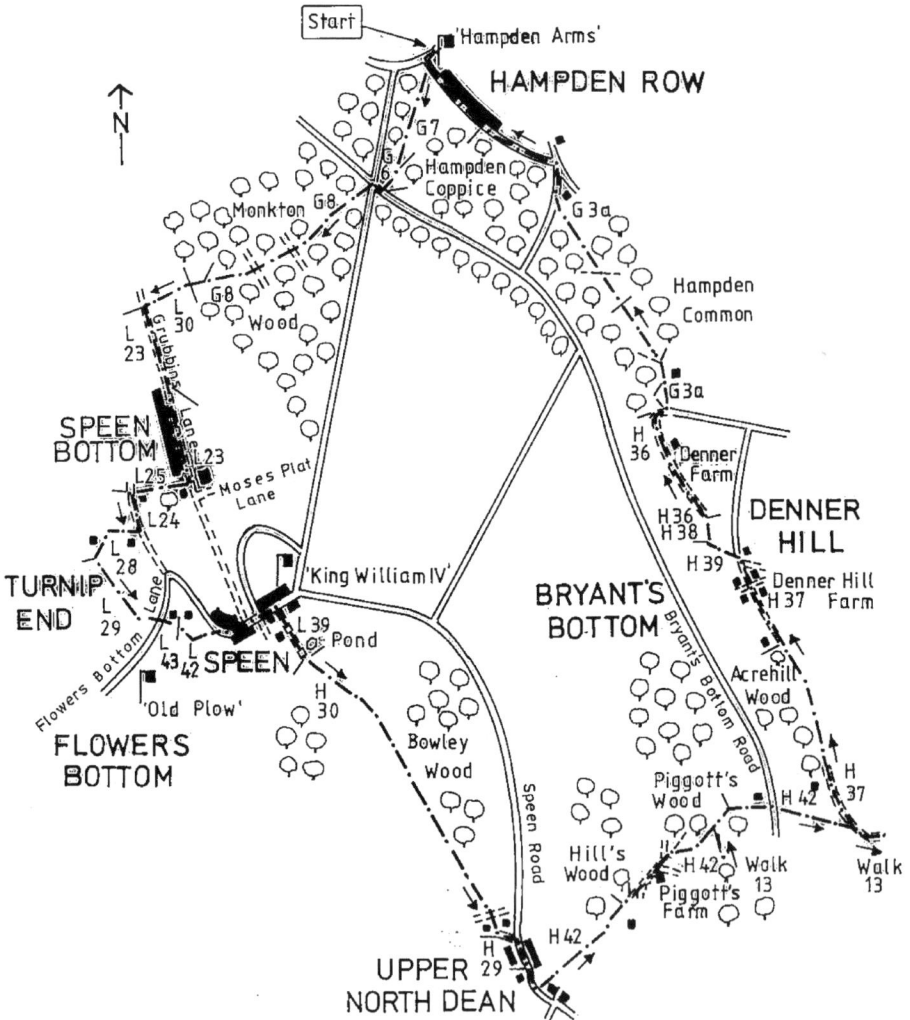

Start

'Hampden Arms'

HAMPDEN ROW

↑N—

G7

Hampden
Coppice

Monkton G8

G3a

G8 Wood
L 30
L 23

Grubbins Lane

Hampden
Common

G3a

H 36

Denner
Farm

SPEEN
BOTTOM L 23
L 25
L 24

Moses Plat
Lane

H 36
H 38
H 39

DENNER
HILL

TURNIP
END L 28
L 29

Lane

'King William IV'

L 39
L 43 L 42 Pond

SPEEN

Flowers Bottom

'Old Plow'

H 30

BRYANT'S
BOTTOM

Bryant's Bottom Road

Denner Hill
H 37 Farm

Acrehill
Wood

FLOWERS
BOTTOM

Bowley
Wood

Speen Road

Piggott's
Wood

H 42

H 37

Hill's
Wood

H 42 Walk
13

Walk
13

Piggott's
Farm

H 42

H 29

UPPER
NORTH DEAN

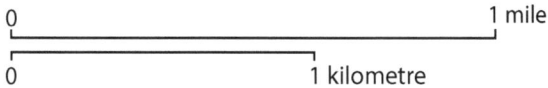

0   1 mile

0   1 kilometre

72

Starting with your back to the 'Hampden Arms' at Hampden Row, turn left to reach a crossroads, then left again. By a bus stop, turn right onto path G7 along the edge of the cricket field. At the far side of the field, go straight on through a hedge gap to cross a stile into a wood called Hampden Coppice. Now take a path near the right-hand edge of the wood downhill, disregarding all branching paths to the left (later on path G6) to reach a road. Turn right onto this road and at a crossroads, bear half left onto bridleway G8 through a fence gap into Monkton Wood. Just inside the wood, go through a squeeze-stile in the right-hand fence flanking this bridleway and take a segregated footpath beside the fenced bridleway for nearly half a mile. Just before reaching a field ahead, go through a squeeze-stile to rejoin the bridleway. Now keep straight on, ignoring crossing paths and leaving Monkton Wood by fenced bridleway L30. On reaching a rough road called Grubbins Lane (restricted byway L23), turn left and follow it for a third of a mile. Opposite a corrugated iron barn, just before the junction with Moses Plat Lane, turn right onto path L25, at first between buildings and then between fences, and follow it downhill, soon entering scrubland and descending some steps before dropping between a hedge and a fence to another rough road (restricted byway L24) in Highwood Bottom.

Turn left onto this road and after about 130 yards, by the gate to a mobile home, turn right onto narrow path L28 between a hedge and a fence to cross a stile. Now follow a right-hand hedge uphill, crossing another stile. Near the top, bear half left and continue to follow the hedge, crossing a further stile, then reaching a stile in the right-hand hedge leading to the hamlet of Turnip End. Do **not** cross this stile, but, instead, turn left onto path L29, crossing the field and descending towards a large pylon in the hedge right of Flowers Bottom Farm, keeping right of a fence and eventually crossing a stile in it. Now continue downhill, crossing two more stiles to reach Flowers Bottom Lane. Cross this road and a stile opposite onto path L43, then take a fenced path, crossing a stile and passing through a gate. Now take path L42, following a power-line straight on uphill to a stile, then continue to a gate and stile onto a road at Speen.

Turn right onto this road and having passed Studridge Lane to your left, at a slight left-hand bend, turn right again into Water Lane (path L39). Where its macadam surface ends, cross a stile by a gate and take a rough track straight on, crossing a second stile by double gates and continuing to a third stile and gate by an attractive duckpond. Cross this stile and take path H30 straight on, disregarding a gate and stile to your left and following a left-hand fence for a third of a mile, ignoring a further stile in it and eventually crossing a stile by a New Zealand (barbed-wire) gate. Now go straight on, gradually nearing Bowley Wood to your left. Having joined the edge of the wood, follow it, soon crossing a stile, then follow a left-hand hedge straight on downhill to cross a farm road. Here continue, crossing a stile by a gate, following a left-hand hedge and passing left of a pair of barns to reach a stile and gate into a lane (path H29), which leads you out to Speen Road at Upper North Dean.

Turn right onto this road. Soon after the end of the houses on the right, turn left onto enclosed path H42, soon crossing a stile. Now follow a left-hand hedge uphill to cross a stile into the corner of Hill's Wood. Here take a path along the inside edge of the wood, continuing uphill and ignoring all branching paths to the left, until the path leaves the wood and joins a macadam drive. Take this drive (still path H42) straight on past Piggott's Farm, ignoring a branching drive to the right. By a galvanised left-hand gate just before Piggott's Wood, fork slightly right off the drive into the wood. Where the path forks, bear right and take a well-defined path downhill through the wood, ignoring all branching and crossing paths, **joining Walk 13** and eventually crossing a stile. Now follow a left-hand hedge straight on downhill to cross a stile by a gate onto Bryant's Bottom Road.

Having crossed a stile by a gate opposite, bear half right up a steep bank to cross a stile by a gate at the corner of a garden hedge. Now bear half right to cross a stile leading to a macadam drive. **Leaving Walk 13 again**, turn left onto this drive (bridleway H37) and follow it to its end near Denner Hill House. Here go straight on through white gates into a narrow bridleway which later widens into a track. Follow this straight on for half a mile past Denner Hill Farm to the end of a macadam road at the hamlet of Denner Hill.

Here, opposite a right-hand cottage, turn left through a kissing-gate by a gate onto path H39, bearing half right across a field to a small gate in a hedge gap. Now turn right onto path H38, following a right-hand hedge to gates into the next field. Here take path H36, bearing slightly left to cross a stile by a gate left of farm buildings at Denner Farm. Now follow a drive past the farm, turning right where the drive does to reach gates leading to the end of a road. Go through these gates and turn left over a stile by gates onto path G3a into scrubland on Hampden Common. Now follow a waymarked path across this confusing common. At a waymarked fork, take the left-hand option straight on, then, at a crossways, ignore a crossing path and go straight on. Soon after this, in a clearing on a slight rise, take the right-hand fork and go straight on to another clearing. Go straight on to the far end of this clearing where you reach a stony track leading to gates and a stile then continuing along a macadam drive to a road. Turn right onto this, then bear left at a double junction and follow the road for a third of a mile back to the ´Hampden Arms`.

WALK 16   Whiteleaf Hill

Length of Walk: 6.0 miles / 9.6 Km
Starting Point: Whiteleaf Hill car park.
Grid Ref: SP824035
Maps: OS Landranger Sheet 165
OS Explorer Sheet 181 (or old Sheet 2)
Chiltern Society FP Map No.3
How to get there / Parking: Whiteleaf Hill car park, 1 mile east
of Princes Risborough, may be reached from the town by
taking the A4010 towards Aylesbury to Monks Risborough,
then turning right onto a road signposted to Whiteleaf and
Hampden. Take this road straight on up Whiteleaf Hill to a
left-hand car park near the top.

Whiteleaf Hill, a wooded hill on the Chiltern escarpment above
Princes Risborough, is noteworthy for the large chalk cross cut into
the turf on the hillside. Although there is some doubt as to its
antiquity, the consensus of expert opinion seems to be that it is of
Saxon or even Ancient British origin. On a clear day, this cross is
visible for at least 20 miles.

The walk takes you through the heavily-wooded escarpment
backland to Buckmoorend near Chequers, the Prime Minister's
country retreat in the upper part of Hampden Bottom. It then
returns by way of the escarpment using parts of the Ridgeway and
taking in Pulpit Hill, the secluded leafy hamlet of Lower Cadsden
and the summit of Whiteleaf Hill with its fine views across the Vale
of Aylesbury, where Whiteleaf Cross can be seen from above.

Starting from the vehicular entrance to Whiteleaf Hill car park, head
westwards through the car park, then take the right-hand gravel path into
woodland. On reaching a wide crossing stone track (bridleway R13),
turn right onto it joining the Ridgeway. After 200 yards, at a signposted
crossways, leaving the Ridgeway, turn sharp right onto bridleway R21a,
following the inside edge of a wood called The Hangings for a third of a
mile. Ignore two waymarked branching permissive paths to your left,
then, where the bridleway forks and the right-hand option begins a
gradual climb, go left past an anti-horse barrier onto path R22,
descending slowly. Eventually the path bears right and climbs to a T-
junction. Here turn left onto bridleway R23, following it downhill and

WALK 16

76

ignoring a crossing track. At a waymarked fork, bear right, then, at a second, take path R51 straight on through a fence gap into Sergeant's Wood. On emerging into a wide clearing beneath a power line, keep straight on, eventually reaching a stile by double gates at Solinger Farm. Here turn right onto a macadam drive (still path R51) and follow it downhill. In the valley bottom, continue to follow the drive which bears left. After a quarter mile, it bears right, passes through a copse called Little Boy's Heath and (now as path G61) reaches a road in Hampden Bottom. Cross the road bearing slightly right and take path E58, a rough track virtually opposite, to Hampden Chase (formerly Dirtywood Farm). At the old farm, ignore a branching permissive path to your left, then fork left through a gate and bear right, passing left of the house, then continuing through a hedge gap. Now follow the right-hand hedge uphill, passing through a small gate and continuing to a gap which leads you into a corner of Widnell Wood. Inside the wood, take the waymarked path uphill, ignoring a branching path to the right, then, at a fork, bear right. At a waymarked junction near the top of the hill, turn sharp left and take waymarked woodland path E57 for a third of a mile ignoring a branching path to your left. On reaching crossing path E55a along the inside edge of Hengrove Wood, turn right onto it, climbing slowly. After 100 yards at a fork, bear right, climbing for a further 50 yards to a five-way junction. Here turn left onto path E56 and follow it to a stile by gates onto a narrow road. Now turn left onto this road and follow it for some 300 yards to the edge of Buckmoorend.

Just before the first left-hand cottage, turn left through a hedge gap onto path E54 and follow a right-hand garden hedge past the garden. Where this hedge turns right, leave it and bear slightly right across the field to a gap roughly in the middle of the belt of trees ahead. Go through this gap, then turn left onto bridleway E79, soon reaching a road. Cross this and take bridleway E30 opposite along a rough track leading to a gate into a field. Do **not** enter this field, but bear slightly right along a fenced bridleway leading you into a finger of Pond Wood. Now take an obvious bridleway through the wood. After a quarter mile, on reaching a plantation, take the waymarked bridleway, bearing left, then later right (now on bridleway K46) and reaching crossing bridleway K40b. Turn right onto this and follow it straight on for three-quarters of a mile (later on bridleway E62), ignoring all branching tracks and paths. After more than half a mile, near the top of Pulpit Hill (formerly called ˊBullpit Hillˋ), your track (now bridleway K40a) leaves Pulpit Wood and briefly permits you a fine view of the Vale of Aylesbury before you start to descend in a gully through scrubland.

A few yards past a right-hand kissing-gate, where you rejoin the Ridgeway, turn left onto path K42a over the bank of the gully, then descend to a kissing-gate. Go through this gate, then keep straight on across a dip. On the far side of the dip, join the edge of a left-hand belt of thick scrub concealing the remains of an old fenceline and follow it straight on for some 250 yards, ignoring a crossing path and reaching a kissing-gate into slightly sunken crossing bridleway K41. Here, leaving the Ridgeway, bear half right onto path K42, passing through a belt of scrub and a kissing-gate and bearing slightly left across a field to two kissing-gates left of a group of pines ahead. Go through these gates into a fenced path and follow it steeply downhill to a kissing-gate onto Cadsdean Road. Cross the road and a stile by a gate opposite onto path R20 which leads you onto a golf course. (Beware of driving golfers!) Now follow a left-hand hedge uphill along the edge of the golf course. On reaching a high protective screen, keep left of it, then, at a corner of a garden hedge, turn left over a stile and take enclosed path R19a over a rise then downhill to Lower Cadsden.

Here, rejoining the Ridgeway, turn right onto the side-road and follow it past the 'Plough', originally opened for the local chair bodgers working in the woods, to reach the entrance to the pub car park. Now turn right, following the Ridgeway (bridleway R18b) uphill through Giles Wood. After some 70 yards, go left at a fork, pass through a kissing-gate by a gate and take path R14a (later R14), bearing right at a fork, ignoring a crossing path and climbing through the woods for nearly half a mile until you emerge by a kissing-gate into the hilltop clearing directly above Whiteleaf Cross. Now turn left onto bridleway R13a (later R13), passing through gates and taking a stone track through woodland along the ridgetop for a quarter mile to Whiteleaf Hill car park.

WALK 17   Princes Risborough

Length of Walk: 6.1 miles / 9.9 Km
Starting Point: Market Hall, Princes Risborough.
Grid Ref: SP807035
Maps: OS Landranger Sheet 165
OS Explorer Sheet 181 (or old Sheet 2)
Chiltern Society FP Maps Nos. 3 & 7
Parking: Princes Risborough offers adequate facilities for on-
or off-street parking including a car park west of the church.

Princes Risborough, originally known as Great Risborough, in the
Risborough Gap in the Chiltern escarpment, derives the first part of
its name from the Black Prince, who reputedly built a castle or
palace here. Its royal connections, however, go back to before the
Norman conquest as the manor was once held by Earl Harold, who
briefly became King Harold in 1066 before being defeated and killed
at the Battle of Hastings. For many centuries Princes Risborough
was a small market town and this has left its mark in the wealth of
attractive houses, cottages and shops around the Market Hall, which
itself was built in 1824. The church dates mainly from the thirteenth
century, but its tower had to be rebuilt in 1804 following the collapse
of its predecessor and only gained its spire in 1907, while its
fifteenth-century former rectory known as Monks Staithe was once
home to the aviation pioneer, Amy Johnson. Since World War II,
however, the town has become swamped with insensitive modern
development leaving its centre as a pleasant oasis in the middle of a
suburban desert.

The walk leaves the town behind after half a mile and leads you
over rolling open foothills with fine views across the Risborough Gap
and up to Lacey Green with its windmill. It then follows the Chiltern
Way for some distance across the upland plateau with open fields at
first and a wealth of peaceful woodland later, before leaving the Way
and descending Kop Hill with its extensive views to reach Princes
Risborough.

Starting from the Market Hall in the centre of Princes Risborough, take
the High Street southeastwards. At a T-junction with the A4010, turn
right onto it and after about 200 yards, just past a filling station, turn left
onto macadam path R3b, roughly opposite Park Street. Take this path

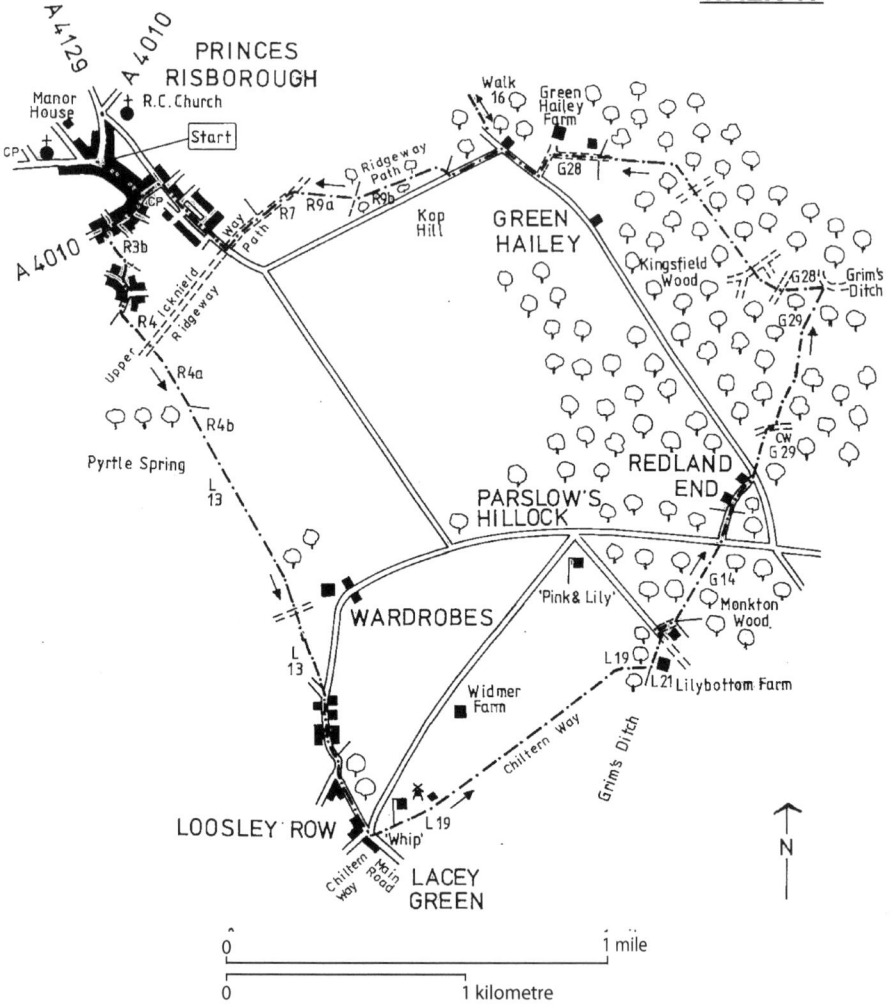

PRINCES RISBOROUGH

Manor House

A 4129
A 4010
A 4010

R.C.Church

Start

CP

CP

R7 R9a R9b

R3b

R4 Icknield

Upper Ridgeway

R4a

R4b

Pyrtle Spring

Way Path

Ridgeway Path

Kop Hill

L 13

Walk 16

GREEN HAILEY

Green Hailey Farm

G28

Kingsfield Wood

G28
G29

Grim's Ditch

CW
G29

REDLAND END

PARSLOW'S HILLOCK

WARDROBES

'Pink & Lily'

G14

Monkton Wood

L 13

Widmer Farm

L19
L21 Lilybottom Farm

Chiltern Way

Grim's Ditch

LOOSLEY ROW

'Whip'

L 19

Chiltern Way
Main Road

LACEY GREEN

N

0   1 mile

0   1 kilometre

80

straight on uphill for some 170 yards to a set of safety barriers, then turn right onto a branching path leading to a bend in Clifford Road. Turn left onto this road and follow it straight on to its end. Here go straight on through a hedge gap into a field , then turn left onto path R4, following the left-hand hedge to reach a hedge gap in the corner of the field leading onto the Upper Icknield Way. Cross this Ancient British road, now a rough lane and part of the Ridgeway, and go through a kissing-gate opposite. Now take path R4a straight on downhill with a fence to your right to the left-hand end of a line of trees shading Pyrtle Spring. Here take path R4b straight on, following a right-hand fence uphill to a hedge gap, then take path L13 straight on over the hill, heading towards the right-hand end of a group of trees to the right of the hamlet of Wardrobes when these come into view, to cross a stile and continue downhill to a second. Now cross this stile and go straight on across a field, climbing to the corner of a hedge, then follow the hedge straight on to a stile. Cross the stile, a macadam drive and another stile opposite and follow a left-hand hedge straight on to another corner of the field. Here turn left over a stile, then bear right across a field to cross another stile. Now bear half left to a stile in the far corner of the field leading to a road junction.

Here join the major road and follow it straight on uphill for nearly half a mile, ignoring a side road to the right. On reaching Lacey Green at the top of the hill, at the ´Whip` crossroads, take Main Road straight on, joining the Chiltern Way, then immediately turn left over a stile by an ornate bus shelter erected in 2002 to mark the Queen's Golden Jubilee, onto path L19, following a left-hand hedge through three fields passing Lacey Green Windmill to your left. This windmill, the oldest surviving smock mill in the country, was originally built at Chesham in 1650, but was dismantled and rebuilt on its present site in 1821. After becoming disused in 1920, the mill became very dilapidated but was painstakingly restored to working order in the 1970s and 1980s by Chiltern Society volunteers.

Where the hedge turns left in the third field, leave it and go straight on across the field to cross a stile under an oak tree, then bear half right across the next field to cross a stile in the far corner. Now take a fenced track straight on to a gate and stile into a field. Here follow the left-hand fence at first, then, where a hedge begins, leave it and go straight on across the field to cross a stile in its far hedge. Now bear half right across the next field to cross a stile into a belt of trees sheltering Grim´s Ditch, an ancient earthwork of unknown origin believed, however, to date from before the Saxon period as ´Grim` is an alternative name for the Germanic god, Wodan, and they are unlikely to have attributed something to a god which they had built themselves. In the trees, turn left onto bridleway L21, following Grim's Ditch to reach a road in Lily Bottom, where the ´Pink & Lily` pub, made famous by the poet Rupert

Brooke, who frequented it before the First World War, is a third of a mile to your left.

Turn left onto this road, then immediately right onto bridleway G14, following a cottage drive at first, then keeping straight on into Monkton Wood. At two forks, take the left-hand option straight on, then go through a fence gap and continue through a plantation, soon passing under a powerline, then bearing left and following the edge of a mature beechwood to a bridlegate and stile leading to a road junction. Here cross the major road and take the road to Redland End and Whiteleaf straight on through the tiny woodland hamlet of Redland End to reach a T-junction.

Here turn left, then, after about 20 yards, turn right over a stile onto path G29, following the bank of Grim's Ditch again through Kingsfield Wood until you reach a crossing track. Now bear right, following waymarks to a waymarked fork where you bear left, leaving the Chiltern Way, and take an obvious path roughly parallel to Grim's Ditch for some 250 yards to leave the wood and enter the corner of a field. Here follow the outside edge of the wood straight on to another field corner where you keep straight on through woodland until you reach a crossing track. Now turn left onto bridleway G28 and follow it for nearly a quarter mile, disregarding two crossing tracks, then descending into a dip. Here keep straight on over one rise and up a second, then, on leaving the wood, take a fenced track uphill, later widening into a farm road. Now take this farm road straight on to reach a gate and stile by Green Hailey Farm. Cross the stile, then turn left onto the farm drive and follow it out to a road.

Turn right onto this road and at a road junction, turn left. After some 250 yards, where the road starts to descend Kop Hill, turn right through a kissing-gate onto path R9b, joining the Ridgeway. At first, keep close to the road, passing left of a large clump of bushes, then continue straight on to a kissing-gate concealed by another clump of bushes. Go through this and keep straight on downhill through scrubland. Disregard a crossing path and now on path R9a, you soon emerge from the thicker scrub by a stile. Now follow a left-hand fence straight on through further scrub and a field to a hedge gap onto the Upper Icknield Way (byway R7). Turn left into this lane and follow it for nearly a quarter mile to New Road on the edge of Princes Risborough. Now, leaving the Ridgeway, turn right onto this road and follow it for a quarter mile to a roundabout. Here turn left, then turn right for the Market Hall.

WALK 18   Bradenham (Smalldean Bottom)

Length of Walk: (A) : 5.5 miles / 8.8 Km
(B) : 2.5 miles / 4.0 Km
(C) : 3.4 miles / 5.4 Km
Starting Point: (A/B/C) :National Trust car park in Smalldean
Bottom.
Grid Ref: SU823990
Maps: OS Landranger Sheet 165
OS Explorer Sheets 172 (or old Sheet 3) (all) &
181 (or old Sheet 2) (A/B only)
Chiltern Society FP Map No.7
How to get there / Parking: The car park in Smalldean Bottom,
4.5 miles northwest of High Wycombe, may be reached from
the town by taking the A40 westwards to the Pedestal round-
about at West Wycombe. Fork right here onto the A4010
for 2.5 miles to the ´Golden Cross` crossroads, then turn
right into a lane signposted Smalldean Lane and follow it
for three-quarters of a mile to an unsignposted right-hand
car park about 200 yards beyond Smalldean Farm.
Notes: Heavy nettle growth may be encountered on Walks A and
B on paths L1 and L3 in summer.

Smalldean Bottom, a peaceful combe leading off the Saunderton
valley into the hills, is followed by a narrow winding lane, at one
point straddled by a farm. The National Trust, which owns the
sizeable Bradenham Estate, has provided a car park here for
walkers, from which all the alternative walks start.

All three walks include some fine views across the wide
Saunderton valley with alternatives A & B passing through open hill
country and visiting the twin villages of Lacey Green and Loosley
Row and alternatives A & C visiting the picturesque village of
Bradenham, one-time home of Disraeli, and returning through
pleasant beechwoods.

Starting from the National Trust car park in Smalldean Bottom,   **Walk C**
turns left along Smalldean Lane and follows it to a right-hand cottage at
Smalldean Farm. Now omit the next three paragraphs.

Walks A and B, however, turn right along Smalldean Lane and after
about 200 yards, turn left through a kissing-gate by a white gate. Now

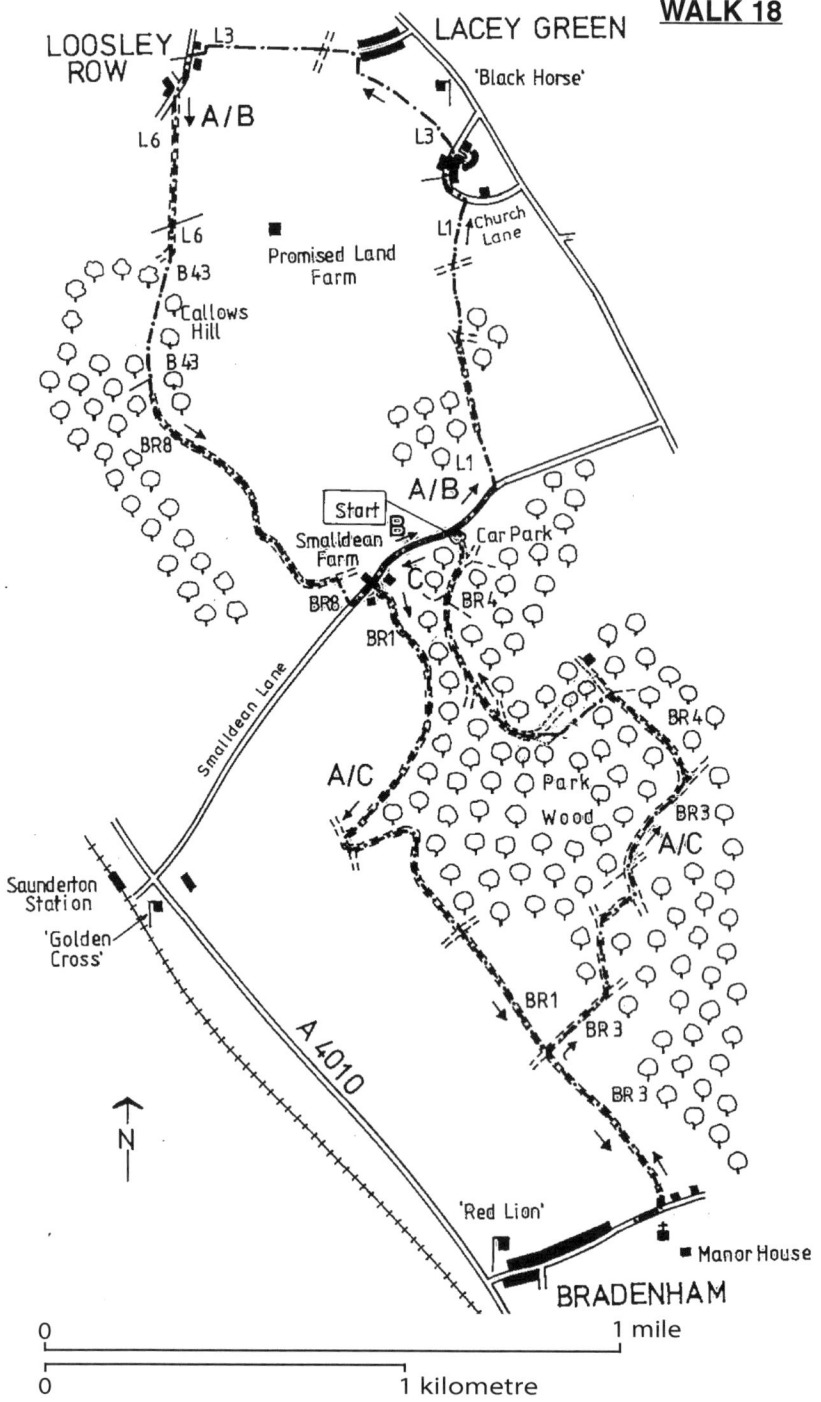

LOOSLEY ROW

LACEY GREEN

L3

'Black Horse'

A/B

L6

L3

L6

B43

L1 Church Lane

Promised Land Farm

Callows Hill

B43

BR8

L1

A/B

Start

Smalldean Farm

Car Park

C

BR4

BR8

BR1

Smalldean Lane

A/C

BR4

Park Wood

BR3

A/C

Saunderton Station

'Golden Cross'

A 4010

BR1

BR3

BR3

N

'Red Lion'

Manor House

BRADENHAM

0   1 mile

0   1 kilometre

84

follow path L1 beside a right-hand hedge to two gates and a kissing-gate. Go through the kissing-gate and take a fenced path straight on. By a right-hand copse, disregard a track to your right and a gate to your left and take a fenced path straight on to a kissing-gate. Go through this gate, cross a farm track and keep straight on through another kissing-gate and along a fenced path to Church Lane at Lacey Green.

Turn left here and follow the road, bending gradually to the right and passing some old cottages. Ignore one footpath to the left, then, opposite Hambye Close, turn left over a stile by a gate onto path L3, bearing half right across a field to cross a stile. Now bear half left across the corner of the next field to another stile, after crossing which a fine view opens out across the Saunderton valley. Bear half right across the corner of this field to cross another stile, then bear half left across the next field to a stile in the far corner leading to a path between hedges, which emerges at the end of a residential road. Still on path L3, turn left here into a gully path downhill to cross a farm road, then go straight on uphill between hedges to cross a stile at the top. Now continue downhill between a hedge and a fence. Eventually the path turns left and then right around a garden fence before emerging at a road in the hillside village of Loosley Row.

Turn left along the road and at a road junction, turn left over a stile by a gate. In so doing, do not fail to look at the embossed metal stile steps, produced by the two hundred year old village forge, giving information about the locality. Now take path L6 along a track beside a left-hand fence with extensive views opening out behind you. At the far end of the field, cross a stile into a belt of woodland and take path B43 straight on along its outside edge with fine views to your right towards Bledlow Ridge and Lodge Hill, then, at the far end of the field, bear slightly left into the wood to reach a gate and stile. Cross the stile, leave the wood and take path BR8, following a left-hand hedge downhill through three fields until you reach the corner of an orchard at Smalldean Farm. Here turn right, passing through a hedge gap and emerging into Smalldean Lane, then turn left and follow this road for about 100 yards to a left-hand cottage.

Here **Walk B** continues straight on along the lane to reach the car park. **Walks A and C** take path BR1 opposite the cottage, passing through a former gateway between a black wooden building and a building with a red-brick gable end. Beyond the farm buildings, take a grassy track, bearing half left and soon following a left-hand fence. On reaching Park Wood, ignore a kissing-gate in its fence and keep straight on along its outside edge. After a further third of a mile, the track reaches a hedge gap at the end of a protruding finger of woodland. Here turn left and at another hedge gap, turn left again (still on path BR1), following the edge of the wood steeply uphill through a kissing-gate by a fieldgate. Near the top of the hill, ignore a kissing-gate into the wood and turn right, following the outside edge of the wood along the contours.

By this point, a fine view has opened out down the valley towards High Wycombe and on rounding a bend, Bradenham, with its manor house and church, comes into view. The manor house, originally built in the mid-sixteenth century, but much altered in the seventeenth and early nineteenth centuries, is principally known today as the one-time home of the writer, Isaac Disraeli and his son Benjamin, later to become Prime Minister. The church, built in about 1100, boasts two of the oldest bells in the country, dating from about 1300, and a plaque to the Christian convert, Isaac Disraeli, while the village around its attractive green has been spared from modern expansion thanks to being owned and preserved by the National Trust.

On passing through more gates, ignore a crossing track entering Park Wood and soon leave the edge of the wood behind. Disregard a second crossing track and keep straight on along path BR3 to two sets of gates leading past the former youth hostel into Bradenham village.

After exploring this attractive little village or visiting the ´Red Lion` a quarter mile to your right, retrace your steps along path BR3 past the former youth hostel, through the two sets of gates and along the track until you reach a crossing lane. Now turn right and take this hedged lane (still path BR3) up the combe until you enter Park Wood. Here turn left onto a grassy track, following the inside edge of the wood uphill. Where the track forks, turn right onto a track downhill and at the bottom, turn left onto a wide track. Follow this track for over a third of a mile, ignoring a crossing permissive bridle track and a branching path to your right. Now on path BR4, bear left and climb until you reach another crossing bridle track. Fork left onto this, then, near the top of the rise, fork right onto a waymarked path, soon joining a wide track merging from your right. At a slight right-hand bend, turn left onto a waymarked path and follow it for nearly half a mile, ignoring all branching paths until you emerge from Park Wood at the car park.

WALK 19   Hughenden

Length of Walk: 6.3 miles / 10.1 Km
Starting Point: National Trust car park at Hughenden Manor.
Grid Ref: SU862955
Maps: OS Landranger Sheet 165
       OS Explorer Sheet 172 (or old Sheet 3)
       Chiltern Society FP Map No.12
How to get there / Parking: Hughenden Manor, 1.5 miles
     north of High Wycombe, may be reached from the town by
     taking the A4128 northwards for 1.5 miles and turning left
     onto a side road signposted to Hughenden Manor and Parish
     Church. Now follow the signposting to the National Trust car
     park.
Notes: Heavy nettle growth may be encountered on paths H54
       and H56 in summer.

Hughenden, formerly ´Hitchenden`, is a name given to a parish, its church and its manor house, but no ancient village of this name exists. The church and nearby manor house both have close links with the Victorian prime minister, Benjamin Disraeli, who owned Hughenden Manor from 1848 until his death in 1881. He entertained Queen Victoria here in 1877 and during his time here, extensively remodelled the eighteenth-century house, the park and the thirteenth-century church according to his own eccentric taste. He is buried in the churchyard and a plaque in his memory was erected near his accustomed pew by Queen Victoria in 1882.

The walk explores some of the ridges and deep valleys on either side of the Hughenden valley, visiting the extensive commons of Downley and Naphill and the hilltop villages of Naphill and Cryers Hill, as well as combining a fair mixture of woodland and open country with fine views.

Starting from the entrance to the National Trust car park, turn right onto bridleway H15 (the continuation of the road), soon passing Hughenden Manor to the left. At the end of the road, take a rough track straight on, dropping through Hanging Wood and bearing right. At a three-way fork, take the central option straight on downhill through the wood, ignoring a crossing path and emerging onto a fenced track along a valley bottom

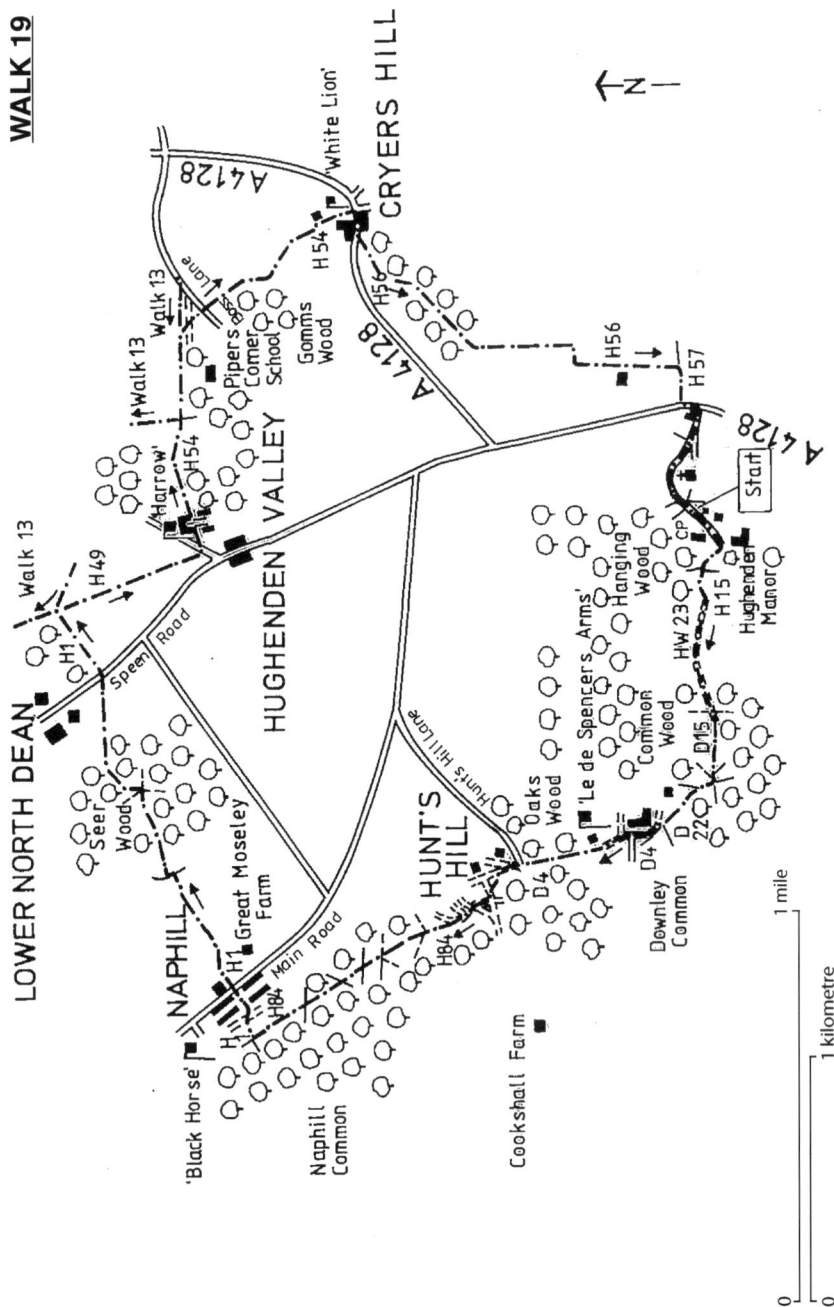

WALK 19

LOWER NORTH DEAN

CRYERS HILL

'White Lion'

A4128

Walk 13

'Harrow'

H54

H54

Pipers Corner School

Gomms Wood

H56

A4128

H56

H57

A4128

Start

CP

Hanging Wood

Hughenden Manor

H15

HW 23

Walk 13

H49

H1

Speen Road

HUGHENDEN VALLEY

'Le de Spencers Arms'

Common Wood

DM5

D 22

D4

D4

Seer Wood

NAPHILL

H1 Great Moseley Farm

H84 Main Road

HUNT'S HILL

Hunt's Hill Lane

Oaks Wood

D4

Downley Common

'Black Horse'

H1

H84

Naphill Common

Cookshall Farm

1 mile

1 kilometre

88

(now on bridleway HW23). After a quarter mile, this enters Common Wood. Here take bridleway D15 straight on along the valley bottom for about 300 yards, disregarding all branching tracks, then, by a large right-hand oak tree with a yellow ´H` painted on it to mark a hydrant, turn right onto bridleway D22. Now follow this uphill, bearing left at a fork and soon emerging onto Downley Common.

Here keep straight on at first, then, just past a marker post, turn right onto crossing path D4 to join a rough track at a bend in it by a lamp post. Take this track straight on past the end of a tarmac road and the ´Le de Spencers Arms` (former title of the Dashwoods of West Wycombe). At the end of the right-hand row of cottages, take a wide path straight on between posts into Oaks Wood and not deviating to right or left, continue past several pits to another set of posts leading out to the end of the macadamed Hunt's Hill Lane on the edge of Naphill. Here take a rough road straight on, bearing left at a fork. Where the gardens to your right end, follow the main track bearing left. After passing under a powerline, turn right onto a crossing track (bridleway H84).

Naphill Common, on which you now are, is noted for its oaks, believed to have been the original Chiltern tree species. By a large concealed pond to your right, keep left, then, at a further fork, keep right and continue ahead for over half a mile. Ignore all crossing or branching tracks and paths, soon passing a large clearing to your right and then continuing along a wide woodland track until you pass through a small clearing ringed with small yew trees. Now look out for a waymarked crossways with a close pair of oaks surrounded by holly to your left, where you turn right onto path H1, soon emerging from Naphill Common opposite No.1, Dene Cottages. Now cross a rough track and take an enclosed path right of this cottage through to Main Road at Naphill.

Cross this road to a kissing-gate opposite, then, still on path H1, pass through a squeeze-stile and follow a left-hand hedge to a holly tree. Here bear slightly right across the field to cross a stile by a gate in the far corner, then go straight on across a field, keeping right of three oak trees, to reach a hedge gap. Now follow a left-hand hedge straight on through a further field to a corner of Seer Wood. Here bear half left into the wood, then bear slightly right onto an obvious path downhill into a valley bottom. Just past a large clump of holly bushes, bear half left and take a winding path to cross a stile at the edge of the wood. Now bear slightly right across a field, ignoring a stile in the right-hand hedge and heading for a gate by a cattle trough just beyond the far end of the hedge, then bear half left across the next field to a stile near the right-hand end of a line of trees at Speen Road near Lower North Dean. Cross this stile and the road, then go through a gap by double gates opposite and follow a left-hand hedge downhill and up again to a gap in it near the top of a rise leading to a concealed kissing-gate, **where you briefly meet the route of Walk 13**. Here turn sharp right onto path H49, descending the field to a kissing-gate in a hedge gap opposite the 'Harrow` in Hughenden Valley.

Cross the road and take path H54 right of the 'Harrow` through its garden to a kissing-gate. Now take a fenced path uphill, crossing the end of a road, climbing a flight of steps and entering a wood. Follow the fenced path steeply uphill through the wood. On emerging at the top, follow a left-hand fence straight on past an ash thicket until the path again becomes enclosed between fences. Disregard the kissing-gate of a crossing path and **rejoining the reverse direction of Walk 13**, keep straight on until you reach a kissing-gate into a field. Now follow a right-hand hedge to a gate and kissing-gate leading to Piper's Lane by the gates to Piper's Corner School. **Diverging from Walk 13**, cross this road and take path H54 through a gate and kissing-gate opposite, then bear slightly right across a field, passing right of an electricity pole to reach the near end of a short hedge. Now follow its right-hand side to enter Gomm's Wood. In the wood follow the waymarks keeping left at a fork, then, on leaving the wood, follow a left-hand hedge to a gap at the corner of a school fence. Go through this and take a path between the fence and a hedge to the A4128 at Cryers Hill.

Turn right along this road and after the last left-hand house, cross the road and take path H56 through a former gateway. Now take an enclosed path beside a left-hand hedge and line of trees for a quarter mile, passing several fields to your right to enter a belt of trees by a kissing-gate. Here take an obvious path which later leaves the trees behind, turns left and passes between hedges for a quarter mile until you emerge over a stile into a field. Turn right here and follow a right-hand hedge to the corner of the field, then turn left and follow the right-hand hedge past a barn to a hedge gap at the far end of the field. Now drop down into fenced bridleway H57, then turn right and follow it downhill to the A4128. Turn left along this road and after about 70 yards, turn right into the road to Hughenden Church and Manor and follow it back past the church to the National Trust car park.

WALK 20   High Wycombe (The Rye)

Length of Walk: 7.0 miles / 11.3 Km or 8.6 miles / 13.8 Km
Starting Point: Southwest corner of the swimming pool car
park on High Wycombe Rye.
Grid Ref: SU874923
Maps: OS Landranger Sheet 175
OS Explorer Sheet 172 (or old Sheet 3)
Chiltern Society FP Maps Nos. 1 & 13
How to get there / Parking: From High Wycombe town centre,
take the A40 towards London for three-quarters of a mile.
Just after the ´Pheasant` roundabout, turn right into Bassets-
bury Lane and after 300 yards, turn right again to reach the
swimming pool car park. Should the car park be full or
closed, on-street parking is possible in nearby side-streets.

High Wycombe, formerly known as ´Chepping Wycombe`, is today a
sprawling modern industrial town, but was once an exceptionally
attractive rural market town, as its old name suggests. A number of
the buildings which contributed to its former beauty remain, such as
its thirteenth-century church with later additions, the Guildhall
dominating the High Street built by the Earl of Shelburne in 1757
and the octagonal Market Hall built in 1604 and remodelled in 1761,
but many of the others have been demolished or disfigured by
modern shop fronts. Despite all this development, however, a ´green
lung` has been preserved reaching into the town centre in the form
of the town's ancient common, The Rye, and the adjacent parks of
Wycombe Abbey and Daws Hill House.

    The walk, though starting on The Rye less than three-quarters of
a mile from the town centre, is one of surprising beauty, exploring an
´island` of rural tranquillity surrounded by conurbations and major
roads. Having soon left the town behind, it leads you over the high
ridge separating the Wye and Thames valleys, where extensive
beechwoods alternate with fine open views, to the picturesque village
of Little Marlow, where a detour to the banks of the Thames is
possible, the return being by a similar parallel route.

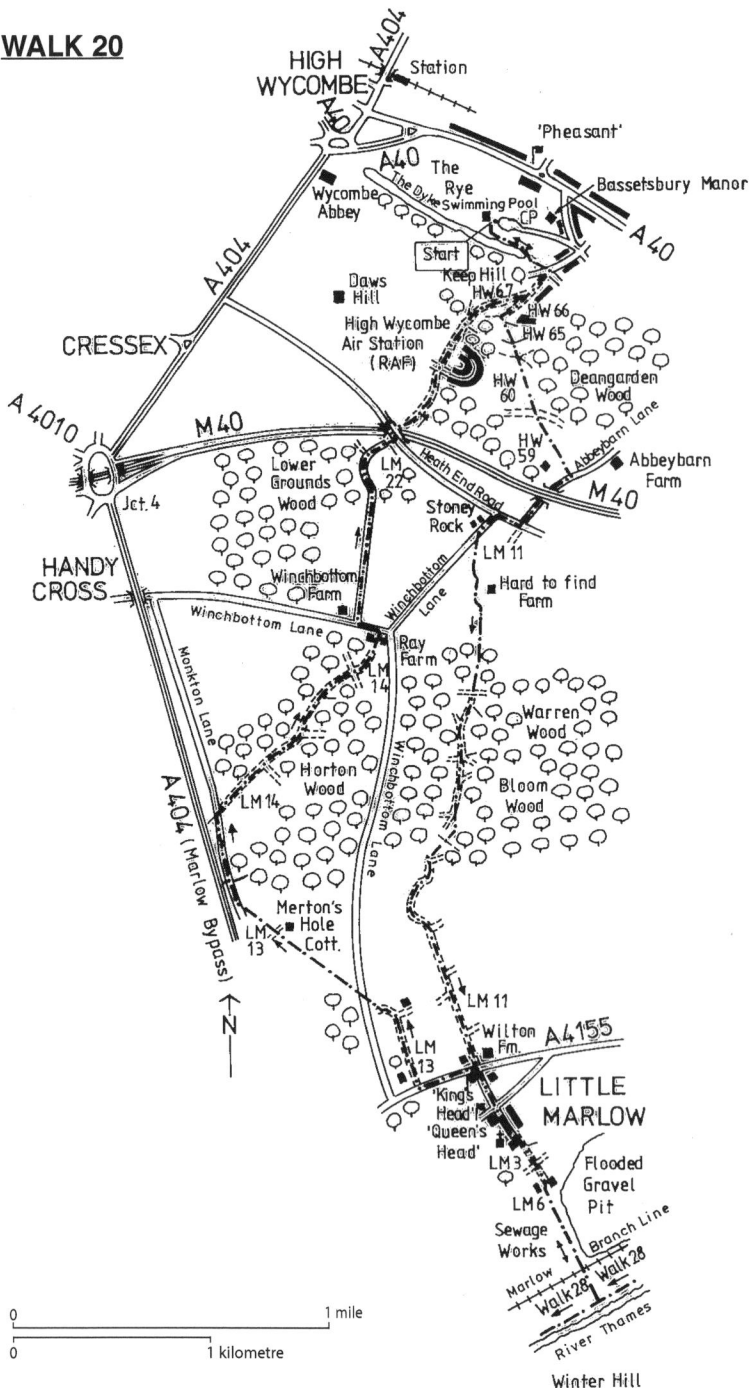

WALK 20

HIGH WYCOMBE

Station

'Pheasant'

A40 The Rye

Wycombe Abbey

The Dyke

Swimming Pool

CP

Bassetsbury Manor

Start

Keep Hill

Daws Hill

HW 67

HW 66

High Wycombe Air Station (RAF)

HW 65

CRESSEX

HW 60

Deangarden Wood

Abbeybarn Lane

HW 59

Abbeybarn Farm

M40

Lower Grounds Wood

LM 22

Heath End Road

Stoney Rock

Jct. 4

HANDY CROSS

Winchbottom Farm

LM 11

Hard to find Farm

Winchbottom Lane

Winchbottom Lane

Ray Farm

LM 14

Warren Wood

Monkton Lane

Horton Wood

Bloom Wood

LM 14

A404 (Marlow Bypass)

Merton's Hole Cott.

LM 13

N

LM 11

Wilton Fm.

A4155

LM 13

LITTLE MARLOW

'King's Head'
'Queen's Head'

LM 3

Flooded Gravel Pit

LM 6

Sewage Works

Branch Line

Marlow

Walk 28 Walk 28

River Thames

Winter Hill

0 ————————————— 1 mile

0 ————————————— 1 kilometre

92

Starting from the southwest (far) corner of the swimming pool car park on The Rye, where the site of a Roman villa was excavated in 1954, take a macadam path to reach the bank of the ornamental lake known as The Dyke. This lake was constructed in the late eighteenth century by the Earl of Shelburne on the line of the old Windsor road as part of the park of Wycombe Abbey. Here turn left along its edge and at the end of the lake, take a terraced path above the river straight on, keeping right at a fork to reach Warrenwood Drive. Now cross this road and take bridleway HW67, a macadam track opposite, uphill. Where the macadam surface ends, fork left onto path HW66, a grassy track along the back of gardens. At the end of the houses, turn left, still following a garden hedge. On reaching a fork, bear right onto path HW65, climbing steeply into Deangarden Wood. Soon ignore two crossing paths and take path HW60 straight on uphill to cross a stile leading out of the wood. Now bear half left, following the outside edge of the wood and soon passing through an outcrop of scrub. On reaching gates by a corner of the wood, go through the kissing-gate and take path HW59 straight on across a field, passing a redundant kissing-gate and continuing towards a wooden electricity pylon to the left of a tall radio mast to reach a stile leading to Abbeybarn Lane.

Turn right onto this road, soon passing under the M40 and reaching a T-junction at Stoney Rock. Here turn right into Heath End Road, then, after 150 yards, turn left into Winchbottom Lane. After about 100 yards, by the second right-hand cottage, turn left through a kissing-gate onto path LM11, following a left-hand hedge with fine views ahead down Winchbottom towards Ashley Hill and to your right across this bottom towards Handy Cross. At the far end of the field, by Hard-to-find Farm, turn left over a stile and follow the left-hand fence to a field corner. Here turn right and follow the left-hand hedge to a stile into Warren Wood.

Now take a woodland path straight on until you reach a crossing track. Cross this track and take a path straight on into regenerating woodland, then, at a fork, bear right, shortly reentering mature beech woods. Here you join a woodland track which merges from your right, then ignore a second track to your right and continue to a waymarked junction. Now, crossing the Chiltern Way, follow the main track bearing left, then almost immediately fork right onto a stone track descending a valley bottom. Where the major track begins to swing to the right, leave it and take a waymarked path (still LM11) straight on, soon reaching a field. Here bear slightly right, following a left-hand hedge with fine views ahead across Marlow towards Winter Hill and Ashley Hill to reach a stile in the hedge, then cross this with a panoramic view opening out with Bourne End backed by Cliveden Woods to your left, Little Marlow and Winter Hill ahead and Marlow backed by Ashley Hill to your right. Now turn right onto a farm track and follow it downhill. Where the track forks by the corner of a right-hand hedge, bear left, passing right of a barn and then following a left-hand hedge to Wilton Farm and the A4155 at Little Marlow opposite the ´King's Head`.

If wishing to explore this attractive village or make a detour to the River Thames, take Church Road straight on into Little Marlow. Of particular interest are the sixteenth-century Manor House, which has been much extended and altered over the centuries, and the twelfth-century church of St. John the Baptist with its fourteenth-century tower where the well-known thriller writer, Edgar Wallace (1875 - 1932) is buried, but there are also a number of typical sixteenth- to eighteenth-century Chiltern cottages which complete the idyllic village setting. If wishing to go to the river, continue to the end of Church Road, then take path LM3, a private road, straight on, later narrowing to footpath LM6 and crossing the Marlow Branch railway to reach the river, the Thames Path and the route of **Walk 28**.

Otherwise, turn right onto the pavement of the A4155, passing the ´King's Head` and following the main road for about 350 yards. At a slight left-hand bend turn right through a hedge gap onto path LM13 following a grassy track beside a left-hand hedge at first then continuing across fields to the site of a former farm. Here, at two track junctions, bear left to head for a copse, then, at the top of a slight rise, leaving the track, bear half right across a field towards a stunted oak tree to reach a gap in the bottom hedge leading to Winchbottom Lane. Turn right onto this road, then immediately left over a stile by a gate and the oak tree and bear half right along a path between new hedges over a rise to reach the drive to a rebuilt farmhouse called Merton's Hole in the next hollow. Now continue uphill with fine views of the Thames valley around Bourne End behind you, to cross a stile by a gate into Monkton Lane.

Here, briefly joining the Chiltern Way, turn right into Monkton Lane and follow it parallel to the A404 Marlow Bypass for a quarter mile, soon leaving the Chiltern Way again and passing part of Horton Wood and a right-hand field. On reaching another part of Horton Wood, turn right over a stile onto path LM14 into the wood. Now take this waymarked path straight on through this pleasant beechwood for three-quarters of a mile, ignoring various crossing and branching tracks and paths. When you finally emerge from the wood at the back of Ray Farm in Winchbottom, the name of which appears to derive from the Old English ´wincel-botm` meaning ´bottom with an angular bend`, take a fenced path straight on between the farm and a farm cottage to reach Winchbottom Lane.

Now turn left onto this road and after 100 yards, just before Winchbottom Farm on the right, turn right into a pleasant narrow lane and follow it up the valley bottom into Lower Grounds Wood. In the wood, ignore a branching private road and where the public road ends, take macadam path LM22, bearing right, then turn immediately left up a flight of steps to reach Heath End Road by its bridge over the M40. Turn left over this bridge, then, at its far end, at a road junction, turn right, then immediately right again onto a fenced macadam path. This path soon leads you into an old green lane which you follow for a third of a mile, disregarding entrances into RAF Daws Hill in the former park of Daws Hill House which flanks both sides of the lane. On entering woodland at Keep Hill, take sunken bridleway HW67 straight on downhill, ignoring branching paths to right and left and looking out for ancient earthworks in the form of a hilltop camp to your left. Near the bottom of the hill, you reach a macadam track used on your outward route and follow this straight on to Warrenwood Drive. Cross this road, bearing half left and retrace your outward route to your starting point.

WALK 21   Tylers Green

Length of Walk: 5.8 miles / 9.3 Km
Starting Point: Tylers Green village hall.
Grid Ref: SU905938
Maps: OS Landranger Sheets 165 & 175
　　　　　OS Explorer Sheet 172 (or old Sheet 3)
　　　　　Chiltern Society FP Map No.6
How to get there / Parking: Tylers Green, 3.5 miles northwest
　　of Beaconsfield, may be reached from the town by taking
　　the B474 towards Hazlemere for 3.7 miles. Three-quarters
　　of a mile beyond the ´Crown` at Penn, turn left into School
　　Road. After a quarter mile, by the ´Queen's Head`, turn right
　　into Church Road for Tylers Green village hall about 100
　　yards along the road on the right. There are small car parks
　　in front of the village hall and down a lane opposite.

**Tylers Green, which derives its name from the fact that the local clay
soil made it a centre for tilemaking in the Middle Ages, once played a
role in European history, as it was here that, in 1796, Edmund Burke
established a school for the children of French royalist refugees.
Historically an outlying common of High Wycombe, around which a
village grew up, Tylers Green is today scarcely more than a suburb
of the town. Nevertheless, the village does retain its attractive green
with its pond and a number of old cottages.**

**The walk soon leaves this outpost of suburbia behind and takes
you at first through peaceful heavily-wooded countryside by way of
the historic Penn House to the attractive village of Penn Street. You
then return through more open countryside by way of Winchmore
Hill and Penn Bottom to Tylers Green.**

Starting from the entrance to Tylers Green village hall, turn right into
Church Road and follow it to the B474. Turn right onto this road and
after 40 yards, by the end of a right-hand parking bay, cross the road and
take path P23 along a macadam drive opposite. Where the drive bears
right to a sports ground, take an enclosed path straight on beside a left-
hand hedge to enter a field. Here go straight on, passing left of two oak
trees, then bear slightly left to the corner of Pugh's Wood. Turn left here
onto path P24, entering the wood and ignoring a branching path to your
right, then take an obvious path downhill, swinging right round the back

of a pit, then left to reach a road. Cross the road, bearing half right, then cross a stile by gates virtually opposite onto path P22. Here take the right-hand of three paths and follow its defined course straight on through Common Wood for two-thirds of a mile, disregarding all branching or crossing tracks, until you eventually reach the road in Penn Bottom.

Turn right onto this road and just before a left-hand bend, turn left over two stiles and take enclosed path P75, soon entering a wood called Charcoal Grove. Some 250 yards into the wood, where the path joins a stony track (path P16) and Penn House can be glimpsed ahead, take the track straight on, soon leaving the wood and continuing along an avenue of trees in the park of Penn House. Penn House was, for centuries, the home of the Penn family, a relative of whom, William Penn, founded Pennsylvania. When the male line died out in 1731, it passed through marriage to the Curzon family of Mayfair fame, now the Earls Howe. The house is reputedly where Händel composed part of his 'Messiah`.

At an entrance to Penn House, join a macadam drive and follow it straight on. At a junction by Garden Cottage, turn left and continue to follow the drive. Just after a right-hand bend in the drive, turn left over a stile onto path P7, following it through a wood to enter a field. Now bear half right across it to a concealed stile right of a cottage which leads you onto a road at Penn Street. Turn left along the road and follow it past the 'Hit or Miss` to a road junction. Here fork left and follow the road across the village green. At a left-hand bend, turn right onto path P77 along the back of the green, passing the cricket pitch and the war memorial to enter woodland. Now keep straight on, soon joining a track and following it straight on to the churchyard gates of Penn Street Church. Built in 1849 by the contemporary Earl Howe, this neo-Gothic church is unusual for the Chilterns in being cross-shaped with a central spire.

By the gates, turn right and take path P1 between hedges out to a road. Turn right along the road and at a right-hand bend, turn left onto path P6 up a drive. By a garage, cross a stile and follow a left-hand hedge straight on. Where the hedge turns left by a cattle trough, turn right across the field to the corner of another hedge, then follow it straight on until you reach a stile in it by an electricity pole. Do **not** cross this stile, but instead bear half left onto path P3, crossing the field to a kissing-gate into the right-hand corner of Priestlands Wood. Go through this and take an obvious path straight on through the wood for a quarter mile to a kissing-gate into a field. Now bear slightly right across the field to a stile and kissing-gate at the corner of a hedge. Negotiate these and take a path between hedges straight on to Whielden Lane at the village of Winchmore Hill.

Cross this road and keeping right of a hedge, follow the edge of the village green straight on uphill to join a road, then continue along it to a crossroads where you cross the Chiltern Way. Here turn right into Fagnall Lane. By the ´Potters Arms`, bear slightly right, leaving the road and taking bridleway P10 across the green, then between a hedge and a wall into a rough lane. Where the lane forks, go right and follow the lane to a road called Horsemoor Lane. Cross this and take path P12 through a hedge gap opposite, keeping straight on across a field to enter a strip of woodland just right of a kink in its edge. In the wood, go straight on to reach crossing path P11. Joining the Chiltern Way, turn left onto this and follow it to a raised macadam drive to Penn House. This mile-long banked track was built in the 1930s by the fifth Earl Howe to practise racing his fleet of cars. Bear left onto this drive and follow it for 250 yards, then, at a left-hand bend, fork right onto a track along the inside edge of Branches Wood, soon joining another track which merges from your left (and **the reverse direction of Walk 25**). On leaving the wood, bear slightly left and take a grassy track downhill beside a right-hand hedge, passing Round Wood to your right, then bearing right to reach a road in Penn Bottom.

Cross this road and take a permissive path through a kissing-gate opposite, then turn right and follow the right-hand hedge round a field corner to another kissing-gate. Go through this and turn left into Crown Lane, passing a copse to your right and reaching Church Knoll with its sarsen stones and small car park. The knoll to your right, on which a house now stands, is thought to be the site of a Saxon church, which would have been more central to Penn parish than the present fourteenth-century building on the ridge to the south.

Now turn right onto path P25 following a gravel track. At a fork keep left, taking a green lane straight on, later with an open field to your right. Ignore a crossing path (**where you part company with Walk 25**), then, just after the second left-hand bend in the hedge, by a marker post, leave the track (and the Chiltern Way) and bear half right across the field to a hedge gap left of a holly tree in the top corner of the field. Here bear slightly left, joining a track and, (now on path P20), following it beside a right-hand hedge to a junction of tracks in a field corner near the fifteenth-century Puttenham Place Farm, where you turn left onto path P24. After 75 yards, by the corner of a farm building, turn right onto path P29, taking a fenced track to join the farm drive. Now follow it to the B474 at Tylers Green. Here cross the main road and take a side-road straight on for a quarter mile to the ´Queen's Head`, then turn right for the village hall.

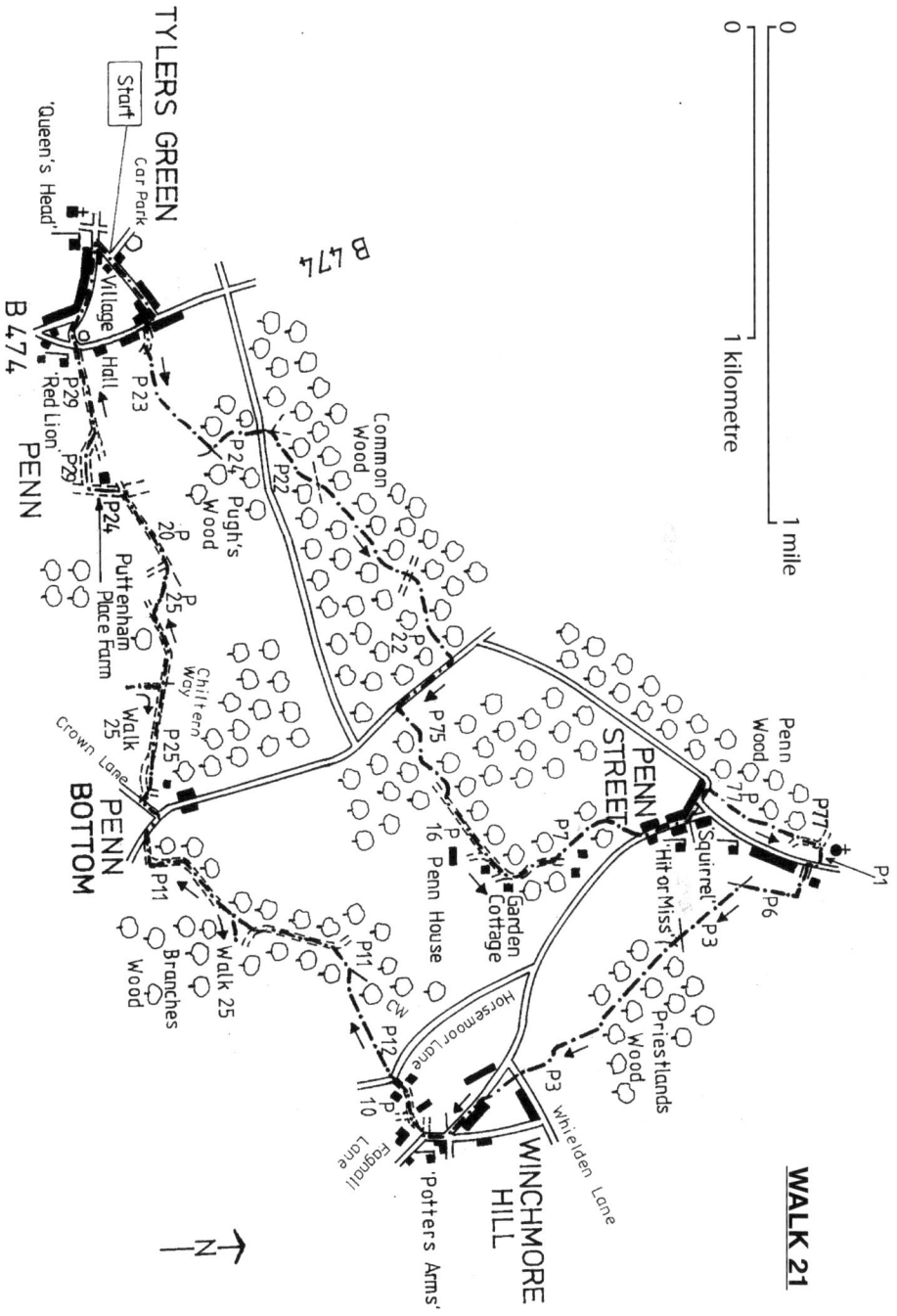

WALK 21

TYLERS GREEN

Start

'Queen's Head'

Car Park

Village

B 474

B 474

Hall

PENN

P 23

P 29

'Red Lion'

P 29

P24

Common Wood

P24

Pugh's Wood

P22

20 P

P24

Puttenham Place Farm

25 P

Chiltern Way

Walk 25

Crown Lane

P25

PENN BOTTOM

P11

Branches Wood

Walk 25

P11

16 Penn House

P15

P22

Garden Cottage

PENN STREET

P3

'Hit or Miss'

'Squirrel' P3

P6

P1

Penn Wood

P11

P17

Horsemoor Lane

P12

P3

Priestlands Wood

10 P

Fagnall Lane

Whielden Lane

WINCHMORE HILL

'Potter's Arms'

N→

0 _____ 1 kilometre

0 _____ 1 mile

99

WALK 22   Seer Green

Length of Walk: 5.9 miles / 9.5 Km
Starting Point: Seer Green & Jordans Station.
Grid Ref: SU965910
Maps: OS Landranger Sheet 175 or 176
OS Explorer Sheet 172 (or old Sheet 3)
Chiltern Society FP Maps Nos. 6, 13 & 22
How to get there / Parking: Seer Green & Jordans Station, 1.4
miles east of Beaconsfield, may be reached from the town by
taking the A355 northwards towards Amersham and turning
right onto a road signposted to Seer Green. Follow this road
for 1.3 miles to a right-hand turn signposted to the station.
Turn right here and fork right again for the station car park.
Alternatively, the walk can be started from Seer Green
village, where on-street parking is possible.
Notes: Heavy nettle growth may be encountered in the summer
in several places.

Seer Green, until 1901, was a small detached hamlet of Farnham
Royal parish over five miles to the south with some 300 inhabitants,
famous for its large cherry orchard which supplied the London
market and gave the locals the Buckinghamshire speciality of cherry
pie. Following the construction in the 1920s of a railway halt on the
Marylebone line, however, the village experienced a tenfold increase
in population to create the suburban-type settlement we find today.
Referred to in the Domesday Book as ´La Sere,` which, as legend has
it, derives from King Arthur's seer, Merlin, resting here on his way
to and from Camelot, Seer Green has an attractive little flint church
with a bellcote built in 1846 and a number of other older buildings
around it.

The walk, which is of a very easy nature, takes you through the
village and visits Hodgemoor Wood. It then skirts Chalfont St. Giles,
passes through parkland at Chalfont Grove and returns by way of
Jordans, famous for its historical Quaker connections.

Starting from the entrance to Seer Green & Jordans Station, cross the
car park and take tarmac path SG1 through a gate and a belt of trees,
soon turning right and descending to cross Longbottom Lane. Now take
fenced macadam path SG1a straight on uphill to cross another road, then

100

continue along fenced macadam path SG1b to reach a road called School Lane at Seer Green. Turn left onto this road and follow it for over a third of a mile, disregarding all side turnings and passing the 'Jolly Cricketers' and the village church.

Just past a garage, turn left into Howard Road. After 50 yards, turn right into Howard Crescent and follow it for about 120 yards to a left-hand bend. Here turn right into path SG12 between a fence and a wall. At the back of the gardens, the path turns left and later right between fences to a stile. Leaving the village behind, cross this stile and, ignoring a stile to your left, bear half left across a field to cross another stile left of the far corner, then turn right onto fenced path SG8. On crossing a stile into a field, follow a right-hand fence through two fields, passing Big Copse. At the far end of the copse, cross a stile and take a fenced path straight on to Rawlings Lane. Turn right onto this road and follow it for some 300 yards, passing Rawlings Farm to the right, which appears to be of sixteenth- or seventeenth-century origin. Having passed a short section of Hodgemoor Wood, at a sharp right-hand bend, cross a stile ahead onto fenced path SG13 rounding two sides of a paddock. Now cross a stile and take a fenced track straight on to reach a large farm building to your left. Here ignore a stile to your right and take path SG22 straight on between a hedge and the building to a stile into Hodgemoor Wood.

Inside the wood, take a winding path straight on along its edge, passing a number of pits and ignoring branching paths to your left. After a quarter mile, on reaching a branching path to your right, turn right, then immediately left through a gap by an anti-horse barrier into a field and take fenced bridleway CG60 along the outside edge of the wood through two fields. Where the bridleway turns left into the wood, leave it and take path CG27 straight on between barriers, following the edge of the wood, then a left-hand hedge. Where its trees peter out, bear half right across the corner of the field to a hedge gap. Go through this and take path CG22, following a fenced track beside a left-hand hedge through one field into a second. Here fork right over a stile and bear half left across the field to a stile and kissing-gate just right of a long low building with rooflights. Go through the kissing-gate and follow a left-hand hedge to a stile into a fenced path. Now continue along this path, crossing a further stile, to reach a road at Three Households on the outskirts of Chalfont St. Giles. (NB If this fenced path is overgrown, you can cross wooden rails in the right-hand fence and walk parallel through a paddock to rejoin path CG22 via a stile on a branching path).

Cross this road, bearing slightly right, and take path CG11 virtually opposite, following a right-hand fence and hedge at first, then between hedges. On passing through a squeeze-stile and reaching a golf course, take an enclosed path straight on for over half a mile, ignoring four

101

crossing golfers' paths, leaving the golf course behind, passing dog kennels to your left and eventually emerging onto a crossing farm track. Here take a fenced path straight on to enter another tree belt, where you ignore a branching path to your right and take path CG12 straight on through the tree belt to a T-junction by an old gate. Here turn left, soon reaching a kissing-gate into Narcot Lane.

Cross this road and turn right along its footway. Where the left-hand footway ends, cross the road again and continue along its right-hand footway for a third of a mile, passing a left-hand turn. Opposite a school sign, turn right through a fence gap onto path CG15 through a belt of trees into a plantation, where you follow a right-hand fence straight on, soon on path CP52. In the trees to your right, you may glimpse Chalfont Grove House, a secret meeting-place for seventeenth-century Quakers. Now ignore a path merging from your left and on reaching a gate by the edge of Grove Wood, pass left of it and follow a right-hand fence to reach a small gate in it. Turn right through this onto path CG14, then bear half left across parkland, disregarding branching paths to your right and entering Pond Warren Wood, then continue through the wood to cross a stile. Now turn left onto path CG16 along the outside edge of the wood to a stile onto a rough macadam drive. Cross this stile, the drive and a kissing-gate slightly left of opposite and follow a right-hand hedge to cross a concealed stile in the corner of the field. Now bear half left, following a right-hand fence across a field. By a pond, bear half right and follow a right-hand hedge to a stile. Cross this and take a path between a hedge and a fence, later transferring to the other side of the hedge to reach a road junction at Jordans.

The road to the left leads down to the Meeting House and Mayflower Barn. Both these seventeenth-century buildings were used by the celebrated early Quakers, Penn (founder of Pennsylvania), Penington and Ellwood (friend of the poet, Milton), for their meetings. Mayflower Barn gained its name from a ship's timber used in its construction believed to come from the Mayflower.

Cross the major road and take Seer Green Lane straight on through Jordans village, purpose-built by the Society of Friends in 1919, disregarding all crossing roads and side turnings. Where the road ends, keep straight on down a rough lane into a valley. Here turn left into hedged bridleway CG54 and follow it straight on to a road junction, then take Farm Lane straight on, soon forking right up the station approach to Seer Green & Jordans Station.

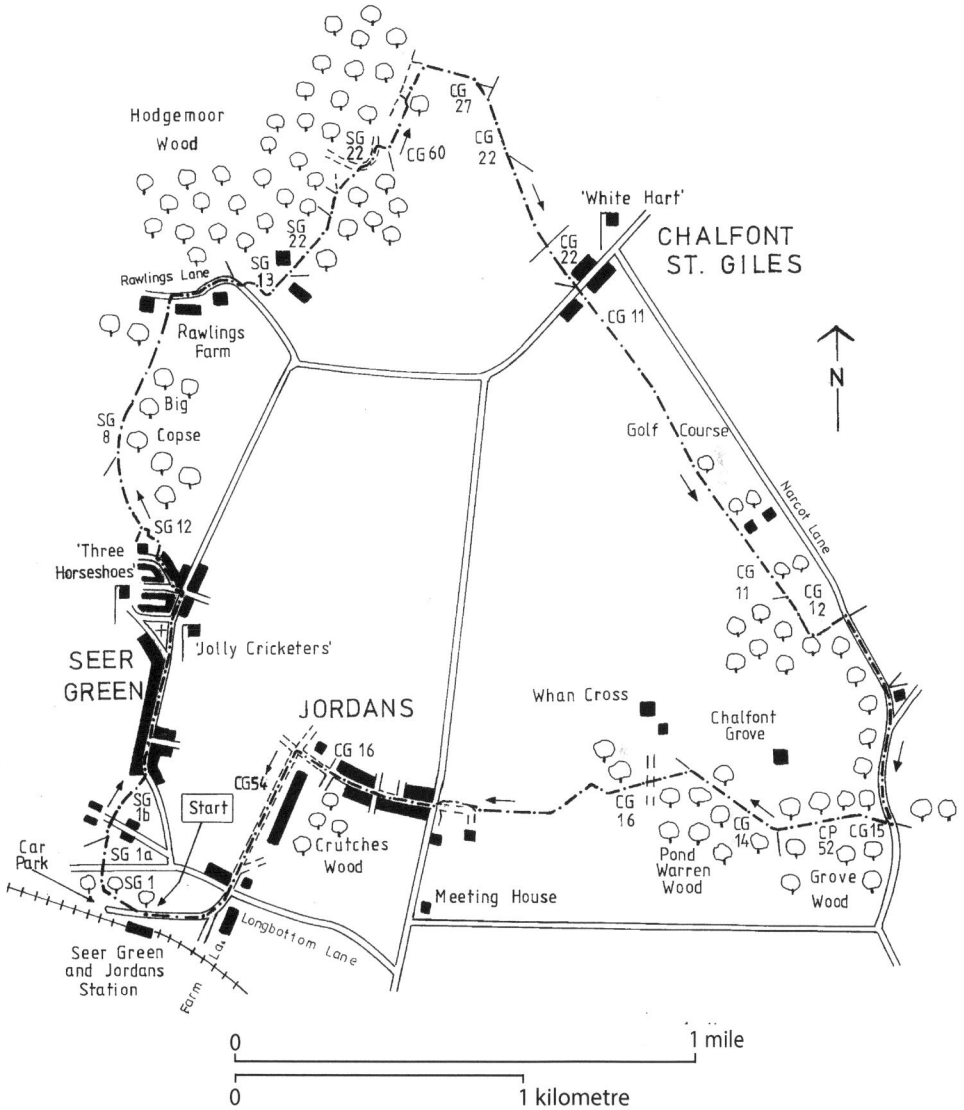

WALK 22

Hodgemoor Wood

CG 27

SG 22

CG 60

CG 22

'White Hart'

CHALFONT ST. GILES

CG 22

CG 11

Rawlings Lane

SG 22

SG 13

Rawlings Farm

N

Big Copse

SG 8

Golf Course

Narcot Lane

SG 12

CG 11

CG 12

'Three Horseshoes'

SEER GREEN

'Jolly Cricketers'

JORDANS

Whan Cross

Chalfont Grove

CG 16

CG 54

CG 16

SG 1b

Start

Crutches Wood

CG 16

CG 14

CP 52

CG 15

Car Park

SG 1a

Grove Wood

SG 1

Meeting House

Pond Warren Wood

Seer Green and Jordans Station

Longbottom Lane

Farm La.

0   1 mile

0   1 kilometre

103

WALK 23   Chalfont St. Giles

Length of Walk: (A) : 7.1 miles / 11.5 Km
                      (B) : 2.4 miles / 3.8 Km
                      (C) : 4.6 miles / 7.4 Km
Starting Point: (A/B) Entrance to public car park in
                      Chalfont St. Giles.
                  (C)   Service road beside A413, 1 mile east
                      of the centre of Amersham Old Town.
Grid Ref: (A/B) SU991937
                  (C)   SU973967
Maps: OS Landranger Sheet 176 or Sheets 165 & 175
         OS Explorer Sheet 172 (or old Sheet 3)
         Chiltern Society FP Map No.6
How to get there / Parking: (A/B) Chalfont St. Giles, 3 miles
southeast of Amersham, may be reached from the town
by taking the A413 towards London to its junction with
the B4442. Here turn right for the village centre where
there is a signposted car park on the right.
(C) From the eastern end of Amersham Bypass, take the
A413 towards London for a third of a mile. Just after a
left-hand bend, turn left into a service road alongside the
A413 where parking is possible.
Notes: Heavy nettle growth may be encountered on paths CG29
(Walks A/B) and CG34 (Walks A/C) in the summer months.

Chalfont St. Giles, despite considerable modern expansion, can still boast a picturesque village centre with its small village green surrounded by attractive little shops, cottages and inns. The church, which is of twelfth-century origin but was remodelled in the fifteenth century and restored by George Street in 1861-3, is linked to the green by an archway beneath part of a sixteenth-century cottage and is famous for its mediæval wall paintings, while in the churchyard is buried the famous circus proprietor, Bertram Mills. The most notable building in the village, however, is Milton's Cottage, where the poet took refuge from the plague in 1665. Built in about 1600, this cottage was where John Milton completed his ´Paradise Lost ` and it was while he was staying here that Thomas Ellwood, who had secured it for Milton, is said to have inspired Milton to write his ´Paradise Regained `.

All three alternative walks explore the attractive section of the Misbourne valley between the Chalfonts and Amersham and offer spectacular views across the valley from the surrounding hills.

Walks A and B start from the entrance to the public car park at Chalfont St. Giles and turn right along the High Street. At a road junction by Costa Coffee, turn right into a road called Up Corner, soon becoming Silver Hill, and follow it uphill past a green and the ´Fox and Hounds`. After about 300 yards, fork right into Dodds Lane and follow it for a quarter mile to a crossroads. Here take Hill Farm Lane (path CG28) straight on uphill, ignoring various entrances to private property. After half a mile, at the top of the hill, just past some farm buildings at the back of Hill Farm, follow the rough road which turns right onto path CG29, joining the Chiltern Way, and soon ends. Here take an obvious path straight on through scrub to a stile where a view of the Misbourne valley opens out ahead. Cross this stile and follow a right-hand hedge downhill, bypassing a redundant stile and crossing a second stile by a gate. Now continue along the other side of the hedge to a gate in it. Here bear slightly right to a stile into a belt of trees ahead. Cross this stile and continue straight on to reach a T-junction of paths with the South Bucks Way by the corner of a fence. Here **Walk B** turns right onto path CG30 (now see the last paragraph), while **Walk A** turns left onto path CG30, leaving the Chiltern Way and joining the South Bucks Way, and follows it, ignoring a branching path to the right, to a stile at the far end of the belt of trees.

Now **Walks A and C** cross this stile and turn right for a few yards to an oak tree. Here turn left, resuming your previous direction, to reach a stile left of an oak tree ahead. Cross this stile and follow a right-hand hedge straight on to a stile into Bottom House Farm Lane with the seventeenth-century Lower Bottom House Farm with its fine timber-framed and weatherboarded buildings to your left and the course of the River Misbourne marked by a line of willows to your right. Cross this road and a stile by a gate opposite onto path A16, then bear slightly right to a stile in a hedge ahead. Having crossed this, keep straight on, passing close to a bend in the river, to reach the corner of a hedge. Here bear slightly left to the corner of a copse, then follow its outside edge to a gate and stile. Cross the stile and follow a right-hand hedge to cross another stile. Now bear slightly left, leaving the hedge and following what is normally a crop-break towards a long red-roofed building at Amersham ahead to reach the corner of a hedge. Here follow the left-hand hedge straight on to a crossing track, Leaving the South Bucks Way, turn right onto this track (path A17) and follow it to a ford and footbridge over the River Misbourne. Cross the footbridge and take path A17a straight on up a sunken green lane to reach the A413. Now cross

this main road and turn left onto the service road in front of some houses opposite.
This is the starting point of Walk C. Now **Walks A and C** follow the service road and later a roadside footway beside the A413 towards Amersham for nearly a quarter mile. Just before reaching another row of houses, turn right down a bank beside a left-hand fence onto path A10 and follow the fence through a field into Stanley Wood. Now keep straight on through the wood along the bottom of a dip to reach the A404 by the gates of Stanley Hill Cemetery. Here do **not** join the main road, but turn right onto path A12 left of the cemetery gates and follow it straight on uphill through the wood, ignoring a gate to the left, to reach a field. In the field, go straight on uphill to the top of the rise with fine views of the Misbourne valley to your right. At the top of the rise, bear half left to a stile just right of where a power-line reaches a hedge ahead. Cross the stile and take path A12a, bearing slightly right across a field and heading for a clump of trees right of a single oak tree in the far hedge, to reach a kissing-gate. Go through this and bear half right, following a right-hand hedge with views of Bendrose Grange to your left, to reach a gate and kissing-gate at the end of an avenue of chestnut trees. Go through the kissing-gate and follow a left-hand hedge to pass through another kissing-gate right of a gate, then follow a left-hand hedge to a stile into fenced path LC1 which leads you past two large houses to Finch Lane on the edge of Little Chalfont.

Turn right into this rough lane, then immediately turn left over a stile by a gate onto path LC2. Now follow a left-hand hedge straight on for a third of a mile to a gate and stile into the end of Coke's Farm Lane, then follow this rough road straight on to Coke's Lane. Here glance over your left shoulder to see a fine sixteenth-century brick and timber barn at Coke's Farm, then turn right onto the road. After about 200 yards, just past the entrance to ´Thatched House`, fork left onto path LC3, a fenced path between gardens leading you onto a golf course where a fine view opens out across the Misbourne valley. Now take path CG34 straight on, passing between greens to enter a corner of Pollards Wood by a white post. In the wood, turn right at a waymarked path junction, then, on reemerging onto the golf course, follow the outside edge of the wood. Where a hedge begins, bear half left, reentering the wood, then, on reemerging, turn left and immedi-ately left again to reenter the wood. After 300 yards, at a corner of the wood at a fork, turn left onto a path with a hedge to your right and the wood to your left, soon reentering woodland. On leaving the wood by the thirteenth green, follow a series of posts along its outside edge, eventually descending into a valley bottom. Here leave the edge of the wood and follow the valley bottom, keeping right of a sunken gully, an area of scrub and a raised green, to

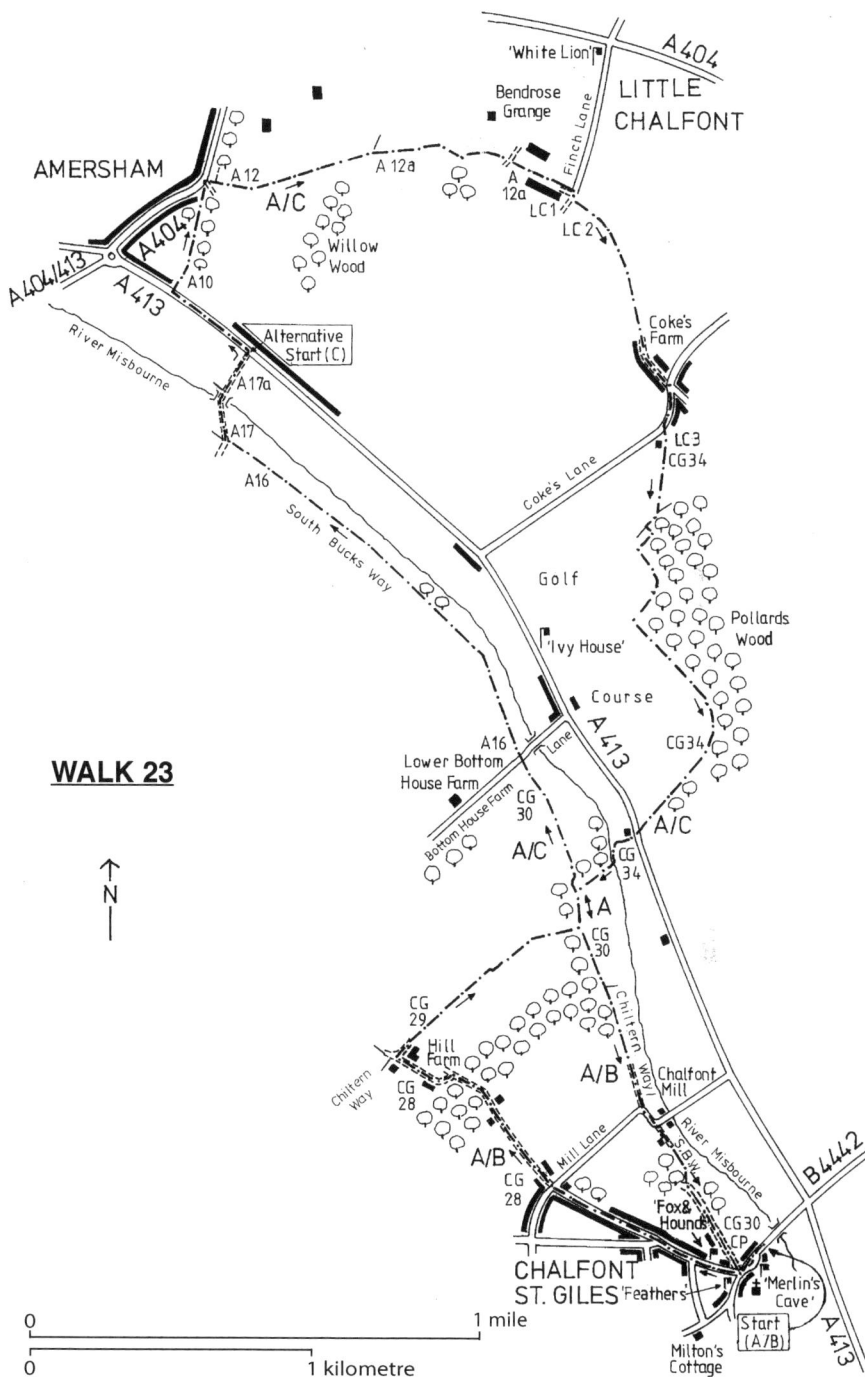

WALK 23

↑
N
|

'White Lion'
Bendrose Grange
LITTLE CHALFONT
A404
Finch Lane

AMERSHAM
A12
A/C
A12a
A12a
LC1
LC2

A404/413
A413
A10
Willow Wood
Alternative Start (C)
A17a
A17
A16
River Misbourne
South Bucks Way

Coke's Farm

Coke's Lane

LC3
CG34

Golf
'Ivy House'
Course
Pollards Wood
CG34

A16
Lower Bottom House Farm
CG 30
A/C
A/C
CG 34
Lane
A413
Bottom House Farm

A
CG 30

CG 29
Hill Farm
CG 28
A/B
Chiltern Way

A/B
CG 28
Mill Lane

Chiltern Way

A/B
Chalfont Mill
River Misbourne
S.B.W.

'Fox & Hounds'
CG30
CP
B4442

CHALFONT ST. GILES
'Feathers'
'Merlin's Cave'
Start (A/B)
A413

Milton's Cottage

0 _____ 1 mile
0 _____ 1 kilometre

107

reach a gate onto the A413.

Cross this road carefully and turn left along its verge, then immediately turn right down a bank and over a stile (still on path CG34). Now follow a right-hand hedge to the bank of the River Misbourne, then turn left and follow it to a stile and footbridge. Turn right over the bridge, then keep straight on along the edge of a belt of trees until you reach a crossing path, part of the South Bucks Way. Here **Walk C** turns right onto path CG30 to a stile (now go back three paragraphs), while **Walk A** turns left onto path CG30 and follows it straight on through the belt of trees, ignoring a branching path to the right and rejoining the Chiltern Way.

Now **Walks A and B** take path CG30 straight on through the belt of trees for a quarter mile. Where the trees eventually peter out, follow a fenced track straight on to reach a bend in Mill Lane. Here go straight on along the road to a left-hand bend, where a detour along the road to your left to the ford past the timber-framed millhouse of Chalfont Mill, reputedly the oldest watermill in the county, is well worthwhile. Otherwise, leave the road at the bend and take a rough track (still path CG30) straight on. The rough track soon narrows to a path leading into a copse. In the copse, follow a left-hand fence at first, then gradually bear right to join a wide tree-lined avenue called Stratton Chase Drive. Now follow this straight on to the village street of Chalfont St. Giles where you leave the Chiltern Way and turn left for your starting point.

WALK 24   Gerrards Cross

Length of Walk: 9.9 miles / 15.9 Km
Starting Point: Gerrards Cross Station.
Grid Ref: TQ002888
Maps: OS Landranger Sheet 176
       OS Explorer Sheet 172
       Chiltern Society FP Map No.22
How to get there / Parking: Due to attempts to prevent rail
    commuters blocking residential roads near the station with
    parked cars, parking in this area is a problem. The pay car
    park at the station can be used if space is available or, in the
    afternoons and at weekends, on-street parking is possible in
    Orchehill Avenue and surrounding streets. Either can be
    reached from the junction of the A40 and B416 by taking
    the B416 towards Amersham. After half a mile, on crossing
    the railway bridge, either turn left for the station and its car
    park or go straight on through the town centre, then, after a
    left-hand bend, take the first turning left which is Orchehill
    Avenue and find a suitable place to park.
Notes: The walk may be muddy in places in wet weather and
    heavy nettle growth may be encountered in several places in
    summer.

Gerrards Cross today is known as a wealthy commuter-belt town just outside London, but, a mere 100 years ago, it consisted of little more than a few cottages scattered around a large common. What changed it was the arrival of the railway in 1906, which gave the village rapid access to London and thus made it become a rural haven for affluent Londoners to move to. Despite this, however, modern planning laws arrived just in time to prevent the town's total absorption into suburbia and therefore, although motorways have since been built to the south and east of Gerrards Cross, there are still a number of surprisingly rural country walks accessible from the town.

    This particular walk is one of great variety exploring the valleys of the rivers Misbourne and Colne with their various lakes and the Grand Union Canal, interspersed with crossing and recrossing the still largely rural ridge separating the two valleys where there is a characteristic Chiltern mix of farm- and woodland. Despite its

length, the route is of a generally easy nature and is ideal for a leisurely day's walk or a long afternoon in the summer months.

Starting from the entrance to Gerrards Cross Station, cross its approach road and take a fenced path opposite uphill. At the top of the rise, turn sharp right onto path GX6a, a macadam path which soon turns left and enters an alleyway, then leads you to a residential road. Turn left onto this road, then almost immediately turn left again onto path GX5, another fenced alleyway leading to Orchehill Avenue. Here turn right and follow this road to the B416. Cross the major road and take a fenced alleyway (path GX4) straight on, crossing a further road and continuing to a third road with a belt of trees opposite. Now cross this road, bearing slightly right to take path GX4 through a fence gap virtually opposite. Follow this obvious path through the belt of trees, keeping right at a fork, then take path CP43 straight on through scrubland, passing a redundant stile and bearing half right down a slope to the A413. Now cross this dual-carriageway and bear slightly left (still on path CP43) to a concealed stile. Having crossed this stile, bear half right with a fine view of Chalfont Park, rebuilt by Col. Charles Churchill, brother-in-law to the eighteenth-century prime minister Horace Walpole, to your left, to cross a stile onto its drive.

Cross another stile opposite, then bear half right across a field to cross a stile in the far corner. Now turn left over a footbridge beside a ford, then take bridleway CP43 straight on along a lane to cross a bridge over the River Misbourne near the weir at the outlet of Chalfont Park Lake. Following restoration work instigated by the Chiltern Society, this lake has once again become an exceptionally attractive feature of the local landscape. At the far end of the bridge, turn left over a stile onto fenced path CP42 and follow it near the shore of the lake for half a mile with views across the lake in places of Chalfont Park House and its modern extension. On emerging onto a golf course, keep straight on, following a line of white posts into a clump of trees right of some sheds. Here cross a macadam track and go straight on over a fairway, through a gap in an area of conifers and across another fairway into a belt of scrub, eventually emerging over a stile onto a service road on the edge of Chalfont St. Peter.

Turn right onto this road and where it turns right and becomes a private road and public footpath CP47, follow it uphill. Where the road turns left, leave it and take path CP47 straight on between hedges to a stile, then keep straight on within an avenue of trees. At the far end of the avenue, cross a stile and turn left onto path CP26, following a left-hand hedge and crossing two stiles to reach a cul-de-sac gravel road. Here keep straight on, soon joining a macadam road called Upway and following it to a T-junction with Joiner's Lane. Turn left onto this road, then immediately right into an alleyway (path CP17). On emerging into a cul-de-sac road, follow it to a T-junction, then turn left into Ninnings Road and at a further T-junction, turn right into Copthall Lane.

Now, at a staggered crossroads, turn left into Denham Lane. Just before a left-hand bend, turn right onto path CP13, a gravel drive, then just before a gate, fork left between concrete posts onto a fenced path and follow this to a stile into a field. Bear half right across this field to a stile right of a hawthorn bush and cherry tree, then keep straight on to a stile at the top of a slight rise into Robert's Wood. In the wood, take an obvious path swinging left and ignoring a branch-ing path to the left, then passing the corner of a field to the right and dropping through holly bushes into a dip. At the bottom of the dip, turn right onto path CP14, soon leaving the wood by a kissing-gate. Now go straight on across a field to a hedge gap ahead, then keep straight on to cross a stile at the corner of a hedge. Now follow a right-hand hedge straight on to a stile leading to Robert's Lane. Bear slightly left across this road to cross a stile virtually opposite, then, on entering a paddock, go straight across it to a stile. Here keep straight on to a gate and kissing-gate leading to a bend in a road at the Hertfordshire boundary just outside the hamlet of Horn Hill.

Do not join the road, but cross the entrance to a bridleway and take path RK5a, bearing slightly right through a belt of trees into a field. Here bear left and follow the belt of trees, later a hedge, until you reach a stile onto Hornhill Road near the M25 bridge. Cross the stile and the bridge and at its far end, turn right over another stile onto path RK5, turning immediately left to follow the back of the roadside hedge for a quarter mile to reach the edge of Maple Cross. Here turn right, following a left-hand hedge round the backs of gardens and then continuing downhill to the A412. Cross this road and take a rough lane (still path RK5) straight on to reach Old Uxbridge Road just outside West Hyde. Turn right onto this road and follow it straight on for nearly two-thirds of a mile through the most southerly village in Hertfordshire, passing the flint Italianate church of St. Thomas of Canterbury and the 'Oaks` and ignoring turnings to right and left. Finally, just past a nursery on the left, turn left onto path RK3, a rough drive which soon narrows to a path and leads you for a quarter mile between attractive gravel lakes. On reaching a car park, follow its right-hand edge to a macadam road, then cross this and a stile and continue along a fenced path to a macadam drive and a further stile. Having crossed these, keep straight on to reach Coppermill Lane by a bridge over the River Colne on the edge of Harefield.

Turn right onto this road, crossing the bridge and passing the 'Coy Carp`, then turn right by the pub onto the Grand Union Canal towpath. Follow the towpath for a quarter mile, then, after crossing a hump-backed bridge, turn right through a gap onto path RK1, following the bank of a stream through a marsh to reach two footbridges. Cross these bridges, then turn right onto a rough road between the stream and a large lake. Follow this for over a third of a mile until you reach the gates of a fenced storage compound. Here turn right over two bridges by the mill-race at Troy Mill to reach Old Uxbridge Road. Turn left onto this road and at its end, go straight on between bollards along the overgrown former continuation of the road, eventually bearing right to join the A412.

Here cross the A412 and turn right, then immediately left onto bridleway RK2/DN3, known as Shire Lane. This green lane leads you uphill on the county boundary to Tilehouse Lane, later with fine views to your right along the Colne valley towards Rickmansworth. Turn left onto this road and follow it for a third of a mile. On entering Great Halings Wood, which in June is ablaze with rhododendron blossom, turn right after 100 yards over a stile onto path DN4a, keeping left at a fork and following this ill-defined winding path through the wood to reach a stile into Halings Lane (bridleway DN4). Turn right onto this macadam road and where its surface ends, take a rough lane straight on. At a T-junction of lanes, turn right, passing Denham Park Farm to your left, then, at a fork, keep left and follow a rough winding lane for nearly half a mile, entering woodland, passing three large ponds and then turning left. After the lane becomes macadamed, just before a hydrant and the drive to ´Blackbush Cottage`, turn right onto narrow woodland path DN4c, following a mossy boundary bank. On reaching a chestnut-paling fence, cross the left-hand ditch and continue along its other side to reach Slade Oak Lane.

Turn left onto this road and just before a bend, turn right onto path DN5, following a left-hand fence into Oakend Wood. Where the fence ends, take path GX2 straight on through the woods to reach the M25 fence. Here turn left and follow the fence to a footbridge over the motorway, then turn right over this bridge. At the far end, turn left to reach a gate, but do **not** go through it. Instead, turn right to follow a fenced path along a belt of trees to a stile. Cross this and follow a fenced path downhill along the edge of a wood called Birch Boughs. Near the bottom corner of the wood, cross a stile, soon entering a field and follow a right-hand hedge downhill through two fields to cross two footbridges over the River Misbourne and a backwater. Now follow a right-hand ditch to a stile onto the A413. Here cross the dual-carriageway to reach a side road, turn right onto it and take the second turning left (Oak End Way). Follow this road uphill for nearly half a mile to reach Packhorse Road. Turn left onto this and just before the railway bridge, turn right for the station.

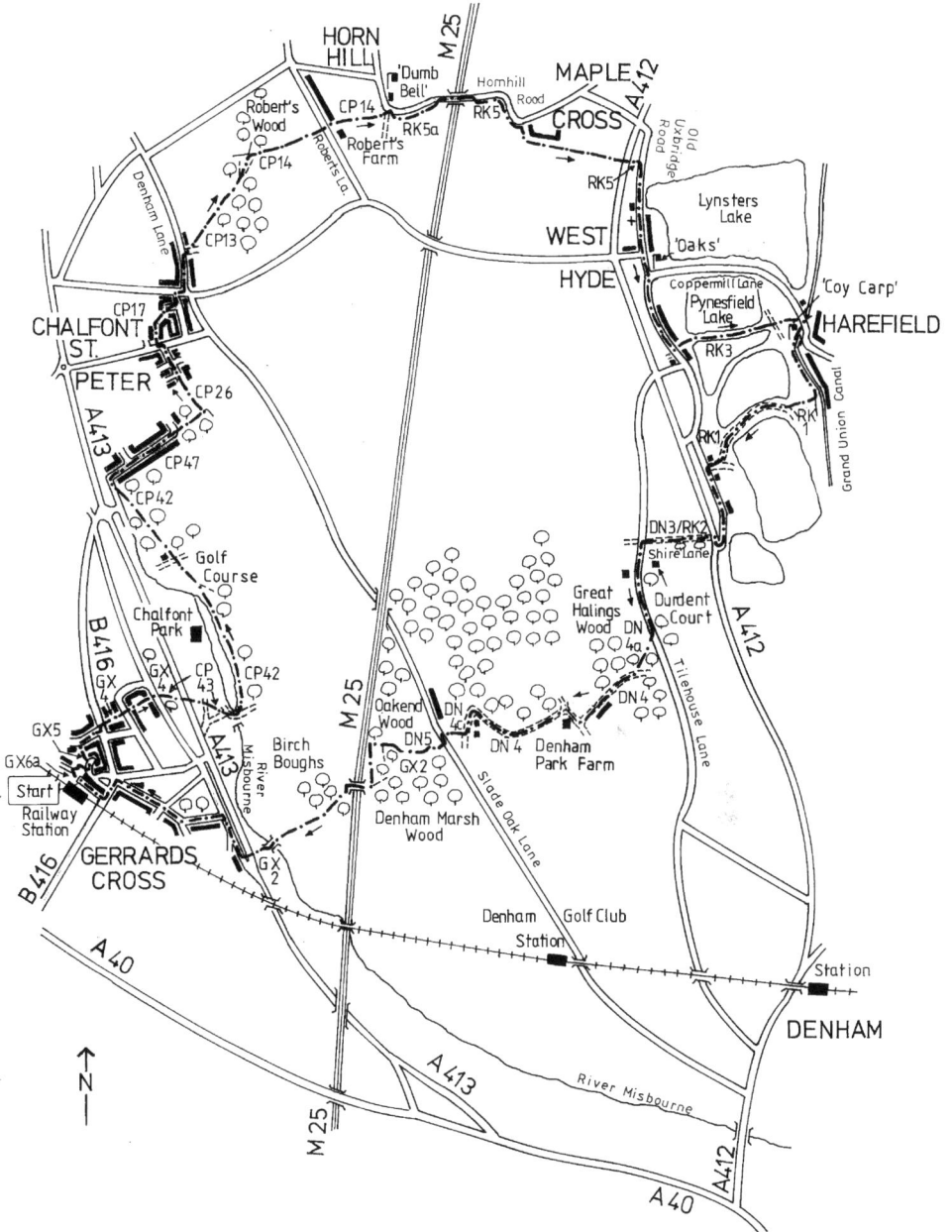

WALK 25   Beaconsfield Station

Length of Walk: 7.5 miles / 12.1 Km
Starting Point: Entrance to north side of Beaconsfield Station.
Grid Ref: SU940912
Maps: OS Landranger Sheet 175
        OS Explorer Sheet 172 (or old Sheet 3)
        Chiltern Society FP Maps Nos. 6 & 13
How to get there / Parking: From the junction of the A40 and
      B474 in Beaconsfield Old Town, take the B474 northwards
      for three-quarters of a mile to Beaconsfield Station, then
      either turn right for the station car park or continue north-
      wards and after a roundabout, take the first turning right
      (Warwick Road) where there is a long-stay car park.
Notes: Heavy nettle growth may be encountered on path P17
      and bridleway B6 in summer.

Beaconsfield Station was opened in 1906 as part of the Great
Western and Great Central Joint Railway, the last main line to be
built into London for a century till the Channel Tunnel rail link. At
the time, it was to the north of the town, but the coming of the
railway, which enabled rapid travel into London and caused a
decline in the importance of the old coach road, also soon resulted in
mushrooming housing development around the station and so today
it is the New Town around the railway station rather than the Old
Town on the A40 which forms the commercial centre of Beaconsfield.
Although the New Town has few historic buildings, it does have one
place of interest in the form of the Bekonscot Model Village with its
extensive model railway and miniature buildings and landscape, all
at a scale of 1:12, which was created many years ago in a large
garden.

     The walk soon leaves the New Town behind and explores the
unspoilt Penn Country to the north with its high ridges, deep valleys
and extensive woodland, visiting Forty Green and the picturesque
hilltop village of Penn and skirting Winchmore Hill and Coleshill
before returning to Beaconsfield.

Starting from the entrance to the north side of Beaconsfield Station, take the approach road westwards to reach Station Road (B474). Here turn right to a roundabout, then take the second turning off it (Reynolds Road) and follow it to a bend. Now leave the road and take enclosed path B1 straight on. At a junction of paths, bear half left and continue for some 250 yards to a further junction. Here turn right, then fork left (still on path B1) to reach a macadam drive. Bear right onto this to reach a cul-de-sac road, then turn left to a road junction. Here turn right, then fork immediately left into an alleyway (still path B1) and follow this, crossing three further roads and becoming path P49, eventually reaching a gate and stile into Hogback Wood. Cross the stile and follow a right-hand fence straight on downhill through the wood into a field and up again to reach a stile near a barn. Having crossed this, take a fenced path to reach Forty Green Road near the telephone box in Forty Green. This small hamlet is principally known for its ancient inn, the ´Royal Standard of England`, which is believed to have been renamed thus in the late seventeenth century to mark its use as a refuge and temporary headquarters by King Charles I during the Civil War.

Turn left onto this road and at a bend, turn right into Brindles Lane, a rough lane uphill past some cottages to reach a stile by double gates at the top end of the lane. Cross the stile and take path P36 straight on across a field to a stile by gates, then bear slightly left to two further stiles leading into Saunder's Wood. Inside the wood, bear left and at a fork, bear left again onto path P39. Now follow the inside edge of the wood, ignoring a branching path to the left, then take path P38 straight on, still following the inside edge of the wood into Corker's Wood, a mature beechwood. On eventually leaving the wood near large gates, take a macadam private road straight on with glimpses of Penn Church between the trees ahead. After a third of a mile, shortly after passing brick buildings to the right concealing Penbury Grove, turn left over a stile onto fenced path P37 with fine views to your left over the hills to the south towards the Thames valley and Maidenhead at first, then continuing to a narrow lane called Paul's Hill. Turn right onto this road and follow it uphill into Penn, where the fourteenth-century church is to your left and picturesque seventeenth-century brick-and-flint cottages with climber roses are to your right.

At a T-junction, turn right onto the B474, passing the seventeenth-century ´Crown`, then, at the far end of its car park, turn sharp left onto path P17, crossing the car park diagonally to its far corner. Here go straight on into Vicarage Wood and follow the obvious winding path downhill for 300 yards. On leaving the wood with a fine view of the remote Penn Bottom ahead, follow a grass crop-break straight on towards an indentation in the edge of Brook Wood downhill to reach a grassy track in the valley bottom. Turn right onto this track (path P25),

joining the Chiltern Way and **the reverse direction of Walk 21**, and follow it for 350 yards, soon with a hedge to your left, to reach a track junction, then take a track straight on to reach Crown Lane.

Turn left onto this road and after 25 yards turn right through a kissing-gate onto a permissive path, bearing left and following the left-hand hedge for 150 yards to another kissing-gate. Go through this, cross a road and go through a gap by gates opposite onto path P11. Now follow a grassy track winding uphill along the edge of Round Wood, then beside a left-hand hedge to enter Branches Wood. At a fork in the wood, (**leaving** the Chiltern Way and **Walk 21**) take the right-hand option (path P13). On reaching a macadam private road, bear half right across it and take a woodland path straight on, eventually emerging into a field by the remains of a stile and a large pit. Walk round the left side of the pit and then go straight on across a field to the left-hand of two hedge gaps leading to Horsemoor Lane about 30 yards left of a tall oak. Cross this road, go through a gap by an old stile opposite and take fenced path P26 along the edge of an orchard. At the far end of the orchard, go through a gap by an old stile and follow a right-hand hedge straight on to a copse. Here turn right through a hedge gap, then turn left past the copse and turn left again through another hedge gap. Now follow a left-hand hedge to the far end of the field. Here turn right through two kissing-gates into a paddock, then turn left onto path P14, crossing the paddock to a kissing-gate by the right-hand end of a hedge. Go through this and bear slightly left across a field to a stile into Fagnall Lane on the edge of Winchmore Hill.

Turn right onto this road and follow it downhill, then, by a fine timber-framed house called ´Lowlands`, take a rising grassy track on the left to reach a concealed stile in the left-hand hedge. Turn left over this stile onto path P86 and follow it uphill beside a right-hand hedge to a stile leading to Coleshill Lane near a road junction. Turn right onto this road, then, at the junction, turn right again and follow the road downhill. After 30 yards turn left up steps and through a small gate onto path CO11 bearing right and following a right-hand hedge to a field corner, then turn left and follow a right-hand hedge downhill. In the valley bottom turn right through a hedge gap, then left into a green lane and take this green lane uphill to pass through a kissing-gate by a gate near Lucking's Farm. Bear slightly right across a paddock to another kissing-gate, then follow a left-hand hedge straight on, ignoring a gate and kissing-gate in it, until you reach the edge of Little Luckings Wood. Do **not** enter the wood, but turn right onto path CO10 following its outside edge. At the far end of the wood, bear slightly right, following a left-hand hedge into a second field, then turn left onto a path into Great Luckings Wood. Just inside the wood, fork left onto a waymarked path through mature beechwoods, winding its way downhill into the valley

WALK 25

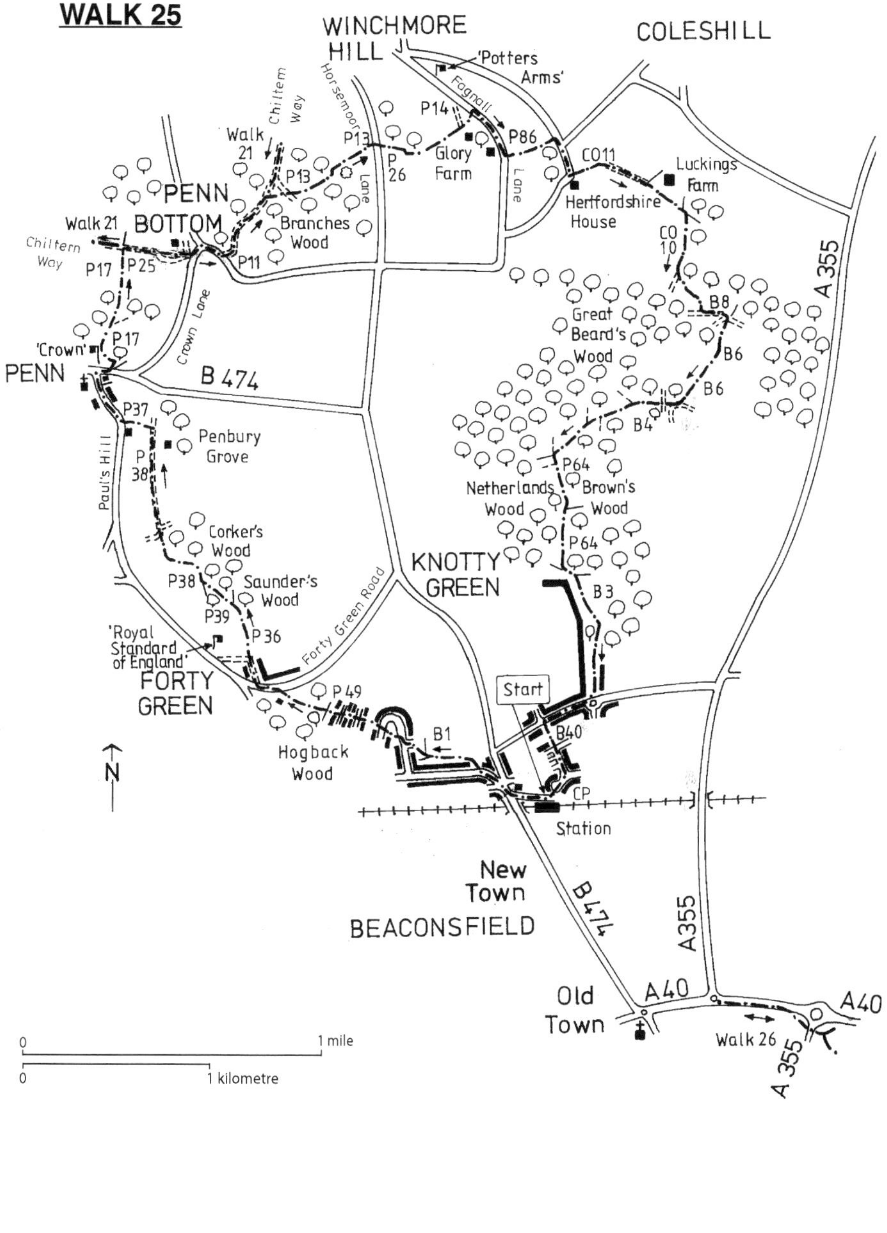

WINCHMORE HILL

COLESHILL

'Potters Arms'

Fagnall

Chiltern Way

Horsemoor Lane

Walk 21

P14

P13

Glory Farm

P86

P13

P26

CO11

Luckings Farm

PENN BOTTOM

Walk 21

Branches Wood

Hertfordshire House

CO 10

Chiltern Way

P17 P25

P11

B8

Crown Lane

Great Beard's Wood

B6

'Crown'

P17

B6

PENN

B 474

B4

A 355

P37

P64

Penbury Grove

Netherlands Wood

Brown's Wood

P38

Paul's Hill

Corker's Wood

P64

P38

Saunder's Wood

KNOTTY GREEN

B3

P39

P36

'Royal Standard of England'

Forty Green Road

FORTY GREEN

Start

P49

B40

Hogback Wood

B1

N

CP

Station

New Town

B 474

A 355

BEACONSFIELD

Old Town

A40

A40

Walk 26

A 355

| 0 | 1 mile |
| 0 | 1 kilometre |

117

bottom.

At a T-junction with a track (bridleway B8), turn left onto it and follow it until you reach a crossways by the corner of a field to your right. Here turn right onto fenced bridleway B6 and follow it uphill, soon leaving the woods behind and reaching a macadam farm road at the top. Turn right, briefly joining this road, then immediately bear slightly right, leaving the road, passing a kissing-gate and crossing two sets of rails onto path B4 entering a wood known as Poland Green. After some 200 yards, at a fork, bear half left onto a waymarked path through Great Beard's Wood. At a second fork, by the corner of a fence, bear half right, descending gradually to reach a waymarked path junction. Here cross a stile and turn left onto path P64, following a left-hand boundary bank along the edge of a mature beechwood. At a path junction, go straight on over a boundary bank into mature beechwoods and continue to follow a left-hand boundary bank, ignoring branching paths to the right. By the rear corner of some gardens, bear slightly left onto path B3, following a right-hand wire-mesh fence. Where the path forks, go straight on between fences through an oakwood. At one point, the left-hand fence ends but soon resumes, then the woods gradually give way to gardens and you emerge into Ledborough Lane on the edge of Beaconsfield.

Turn right along this road, then, just before its junction with Sandelswood End, turn left onto the tree-lined macadam path B40. On reaching a road called St. Michael's Green, follow it straight on past the church of St. Michael and All Angels to a T-junction. Here turn right into Caledon Close and at its end, take a fenced path off the left side of the loop road to reach Beaconsfield Station.

WALK 26   Beaconsfield (Old Town)

Length of Walk: 8.7 miles / 14.0 Km
Starting Point: Small roundabout at junction of A40 (London End) & northbound A355 in Beaconsfield Old Town.
Grid Ref: SU948902
Maps: OS Landranger Sheet 175 (or 176 except 200 yards at start/finish)
OS Explorer Sheet 172 (or old Sheet 3)
Chiltern Society FP Maps Nos. 13 & 22
Parking: Numerous parking spaces are available in London End (A40) or, if full, ample additional spaces can be found in Windsor End near the Church.
Notes: Heavy nettle growth may be encountered in summer, particularly on path B48.

Beaconsfield Old Town, with its profusion of picturesque sixteenth- and seventeenth-century houses, shops and inns, is the epitome of the old Buckinghamshire market town. In 1909, Beaconsfield so captivated the poet, G.K. Chesterton that he decided to move there from London and spent the remaining twenty-seven years of his life living in the town. Three centuries earlier, another poet came to Beaconsfield when Edmund Waller and his mother bought Hall Barn, a large mansion just outside the town, while, in 1769, the political theorist, Edmund Burke, bought the Gregories Estate as a country retreat. Both Waller and Burke lie buried at the heavily-restored fifteenth-century parish church near the roundabout marking the centre of the Old Town.

The walk first has to take you over or under the major new roads which have relieved Beaconsfield of some of its traffic burden, before reaching surprisingly remote and well-wooded Chiltern countryside and the unspoilt village of Hedgerley, which is a mere 20 miles from Central London. From here, you recross the M40 and continue across the spacious Bulstrode Park to skirt Gerrards Cross before returning through more quiet and heavily-wooded Chiltern countryside to Old Beaconsfield.

Starting from the small roundabout at the junction of the A40 (London End) and the northbound A355, take the right-hand foot-way of the A40 eastwards. On approaching Pyebush Roundabout, where the footway ends, fork right onto path B44, following the old line of the road to an underpass under the southbound A355. At its far end, by the disused gates of an industrial site, bear right onto a fenced path, continuing through a tree belt to a stile onto Pyebush Lane. Turn right onto this road and follow it for nearly a third of a mile until you reach the end of the road. Here go straight on past a black metal padlocked gate onto path B48 and continue to the M40 fence, where you turn sharp left along a fenced path beside the motorway for nearly half a mile to reach a flight of steps leading up to a bridge over the motorway.

Turn right over this bridge, then cross Hedgerley Lane and go through gates opposite onto path HE19. Now take a track straight on to cross a stile, then follow a right-hand hedge. At a corner of the hedge, bear half left across the field, passing left of an oak tree and crossing a stile to reach a corner of Cave Wood. Here bear slightly left along the outside edge of the wood to a kissing-gate into the wood in a corner of the field. Now follow an obvious woodland track straight on downhill to a macadam farm road. Turn right onto this road and after some 30 yards, turn left onto a woodland track. Where this track turns right, leave it and take a path straight on, eventually crossing a stile and soon reaching Beaconsfield Common Lane.

Turn right onto this road and after about 50 yards, turn left over a stile by a gate onto path HE5. Now bear half right across the field to a stile by an electricity pole right of Sutton's Wood. Here bear half left across the next field to cross a stile and continue across a third field, passing the left-hand corner of a fenced plantation to reach a gate and kissing-gate by the corner of Sutton's Wood. Now bear left, following the outside edge of the wood. At the far end of the wood, follow a sporadic left-hand hedge along the top of a steep bank, bearing right, then bear half left through a kissing-gate and across a field to a stile in the corner leading to Village Lane in Hedgerley.

Hedgerley, formerly a centre of brickmaking as witnessed by traces of old claypits in the area, has somehow escaped the suburbanisation which has afflicted most villages so close to London and remains a real picture-book country village. Its church was, however, only built in 1852 to replace an earlier building which was demolished, but it contains a number of relics from the old church including a piece of seventeenth-century velvet reputed to be the remains of a cloak given to the church by King Charles II as an altar cloth. Other buildings are much older though, including ´Old Quaker's House`, a timber-framed sixteenth-century building.

Turn right along Village Lane, passing ´Old Quaker's House` and the

'White Horse'. Just past a left-hand duckpond shaded by a fine willow, turn left by Court Farm into a lane (path HE13), **joining the route of Walk 29**. Now follow this out of the village, passing through two sets of gates to reach a gate and kissing-gate near a corner of Church Wood. Here go through the kissing-gate and, **parting company with Walk 29**, follow the outside edge of Church Wood through two fields. Now take a grass track across a third field to gates and stiles. Cross the right-hand stile and follow a left-hand fence to an M40 underpass. At the far end of the underpass, go through a concealed kissing-gate and take path GX23, following a left-hand fence straight on to a gate and stile leading to Hedgerley Lane.

Turn right onto this road and follow it to a right-hand bend, then fork left onto path GX15, going straight on between large brick gateposts into Bulstrode Park. Legend has it that this name arose because Shobington, the Saxon who owned the park at the time of the Norman conquest, and his men routed the Norman troops sent to dispossess him thanks to being mounted on bulls! In the park, take a gravel drive straight on to a gate and kissing-gate where it forks, then bear slightly right off the metalled track onto a worn path leading you to a stile. Cross this and bear slightly right, following a worn path for nearly half a mile to reach a kissing-gate into the end of a cul-de-sac road on the edge of Gerrards Cross called Main Drive. Follow this road past the drive to 'Blue Cedars' and 'Maple Downe', then turn left onto a path between a hedge and a fence (still GX15) and follow it between gardens to the A40 on the edge of Gerrards Cross.

Cross this main road carefully and turn left onto its footway, then turn immediately right onto path GX8 down some concealed steps into a copse. Take the obvious path through the copse, then a fenced path along the edge of a field, eventually emerging at a road junction. Here turn left into Bull Lane and follow it straight on for a third of a mile crossing the railway into Chalfont St. Peter. Where the road forks, turn left into Maltmans Lane and follow it for 300 yards rounding a right-hand bend. At a second right-hand bend, turn left through a kissing-gate onto path CP31, taking a fenced path past a large new house to reach another kissing-gate. Go through this and bear right along a fenced path beside the drive to Parkwood Farm for about 200 yards. On nearing a house, bear right through a hedge gap and follow the fenced path along the edge of a field. By farm buildings, bear slightly left, briefly joining a macadam road, then, where the road turns right into a farmyard, go straight on through a squeeze-stile and take a fenced path to a junction. Here take a hedged path straight on to Layter's Green Lane near Layter's Green.

Turn left onto this road, then immediately right through gates into a wood (still on path CP31). Now take a woodland track for a third of a mile, ignoring a crossing track, then continuing past a right-hand field. At the far end of the field, bear slightly left onto a path dropping gently through the wood. Ignore branching paths to the left and at the far side of the wood, turn left onto path CP28 running along its inside edge. Soon you leave the right-hand field behind and keep straight on through Great Legs Wood, ignoring any branching paths, passing through a kissing-gate under a powerline and then following a right-hand fence downhill to a kissing-gate at the edge of the wood. Now on path CG52, follow a left-hand hedge straight on with a view towards Jordans to your right to reach a kissing-gate, then follow a left-hand fence straight on, passing a copse. By its far end, go through another kissing-gate and continue across a field, ignoring a metal gate and kissing-gate to your left and reaching a kissing-gate leading to a railway footbridge. Now take path CP28 again, crossing the footbridge and passing through a small gate, then ignore a crossing track and bear half right into woodland. After some 60 yards, fork left onto a path through a mature plantation and follow it straight on to reach Potkiln Lane.

Cross this road and go through a kissing-gate opposite and bear half left to a corner of Pitlands Wood by a pylon. Here bear half left again and follow the outside edge of the wood to a small gate in a corner of the field. Now go straight on into the wood initially under a powerline. After some 150 yards, bear slightly right away from the powerline, soon reaching a kissing-gate into Wilton Park. Now take path B17, following a left-hand fence, soon with a playing field to your right. At the far end of the wood to your left, bear half left across grassland to the left-hand corner of a security fence, then bear half left again, initially following the left-hand fence, but then bearing away through the trees on an obvious path to join a right-hand fence. On reaching a macadam drive, cross it and keep straight on behind garages to a footbridge. Cross this and go straight on across an old parkland field to a hedge gap under a powerline, then bear slightly left across the next field to a gap in the A40 fence. Go through this, then cross a culvert and turn right along the bottom of the embankment to a flight of steps, then turn left up the steps to the A40. Now cross this dual-carriageway carefully and take a macadam path (still B17) straight on to reach the entrance to the A355 underpass. Here turn right onto path B44 through the underpass and retrace your steps into Beaconsfield.

WALK 26

123

WALK 27   Wooburn Green

Length of Walk: 6.2 miles / 10.0 Km
Starting Point: Public car park in Red Lion Way, Wooburn
Green.
Grid Ref: SU912885
Maps: OS Landranger Sheet 175
OS Explorer Sheet 172 (or old Sheet 3)
Chiltern Society FP Maps Nos. 13 & 24
How to get there / Parking: Wooburn Green, 2.2 miles south-
west of Beaconsfield, may be reached from High Wycombe
by taking the A40 towards London to the Dreams
Roundabout (M40 : Junction 3), then taking the A4094
towards Wooburn Green, Bourne End and Maidenhead.
Follow this for 1.5 miles to a large village green on the left,
then turn right onto a road signposted to Flackwell Heath.
Now turn right again into Red Lion Way where a free car
park is on your right. (NB This is not to be confused with
the ´Red Lion` car park).
Notes: Heavy nettle growth may be encountered in summer,
particularly on path B19 and parts of the walk tend to be
boggy.

Wooburn Green, although now linked to High Wycombe by
continuous development, has managed to preserve some of its village
character. Set around a well-kept green, the village, which was once
known as ´Bishop's Wooburn`, has a number of attractive inns and
cottages, some of which date from the seventeenth century. The
River Wye, with its willows, flows past the village and there are
green hills on both sides of the valley.
    The walk itself crosses the Wye and scales the ridge to the east,
makes a wide circle on the surprisingly remote hilltop plateau,
ltaking in the hamlets of Burghers Hill and Littleworth Common and
a variety of pleasant countryside in between, and then drops back
down into Wooburn Green.

Starting from the entrance to the public car park in Wooburn Green, turn
left into Red Lion Way, then left again down Whitepit Lane to the
A4094. Cross this road and go straight on across the green into Windsor

Lane, a road leaving the green on the far side. Follow the road out of the village, crossing the River Wye by a narrow hump-backed bridge. At a sharp right-hand bend, turn left up some steps onto path WB23 and cross a stile into a field. Now bear right and follow the hedge uphill to cross a stile into Mill Wood. Here continue parallel to the road but do not join it until reaching a road junction at the top of Windsor Hill. Turn right here, crossing the top of the hill road and entering bridleway WB10 between a fence and a hedge to the left of the entrance to a private road called The Chase. Now follow it, passing between buildings into the end of the village street at Burghers Hill (formerly known as Beggars Hill).

Take this narrow road through the hamlet to a sharp left-hand bend. Turn right here onto bridleway WB9, passing a gabled cottage whose upper storey juts out across the bridleway in a fashion most perilous to horseriders! Just beyond this, turn left and take the fenced bridleway along the edge of Farm Wood. After some 200 yards, disregarding a crossing path, bear half left into the wood. Now follow the bridleway, ignoring branching paths to right and left and then crossing a clearing to reach a bridlegate leading to a road near Hedsor Rectory, onto which you turn left joining the Beeches Way.

At a left-hand bend, turn right into bridleway TP2 between a hedge and the edge of Sheepcote Woods, much of which have been clear-felled. After a quarter mile, by a cottage, the bridleway joins a drive and follows it out to Sheepcote Lane. Cross this road and a footbridge opposite into woodland, then bear left onto path TP28 parallel to the road, later bearing right. Where the path forks, bear left onto path TP21 over a footbridge and cross Wooburn Common Road and a stile opposite onto path TP3. Now follow this path along the inside edge of the copse, then cross a stile out of the wood and a track and take a fenced path straight on across a field. After a quarter mile, cross a stile and take a fenced path along the outside edge of Bristles Wood for a third of a mile (later on path BU17) to reach Littleworth Road at Littleworth Common.

Leaving the Beeches Way, turn left onto this road and follow it for nearly half a mile, ignoring two turnings to the right and passing Dropmore´s Victorian church and the ´Jolly Woodman`. At a right-hand bend in a dip in the road, fork left up path BU20. In a few yards, turn left onto the drive to Hicknaham Farm. By the farm, turn right along a lane, forking left of Hicknaham Plantation. Just past a belt of trees on the left, turn left through a hedge gap onto path BU18 (later path TP1), following the left-hand side of a fence across a field. On reaching a hedge, turn right through a fence gap and follow the hedge (later on path B27) until you reach a road called Green Common Lane.

Go straight on along this road, soon bearing left. About 100 yards beyond this bend, by a holly tree, turn right over a stile onto path B18, bearing slightly right across a field to a stile into a corner of Dipple

Wood. Take an obvious path straight on through the wood to emerge through a gap into a field. Here turn left onto path B19 with a fence and bund enclosing gravel workings to your right and the edge of the wood, later a hedge, to your left. After a third of a mile, on reaching a transverse hedge, turn right still following the fence of the gravel workings and ignoring a stile to your left. On nearing Lillyfee Farm, the track turns right again and leads you into a field, where you bear left along its edge, passing right of some grain silos to reach a farm road. Turn right onto this, then, just past an oak tree, turn left onto a grassy track between a left-hand hedge and the fence of the gravel workings. Where this hedge ends, turn right and follow another track, soon bearing left. On emerging into a field, turn sharp left into a green lane and follow it for 250 yards to Over's Farm, then continue along its drive, passing left of a security gate to reach a narrow road.

Cross the road and a stile and go diagonally across a field to a hedge gap leading to Broad Lane left of the centre of Mill Wood ahead. Here cross the road and take bridleway B19 into the wood, following it (later bridleway WB11) for some 200 yards until reaching a T-junction with a crossing path. Turn left here and after 70 yards, turn right and immediately fork left onto path WB24 and follow this downhill to reach a kissing-gate into a field. Bear half left across the field to a kissing-gate. Go through this and keep straight on across the next field to cross a stile, then descend a slope and steps onto Windsor Hill. From here you retrace your steps to Wooburn Green.

WALK 27

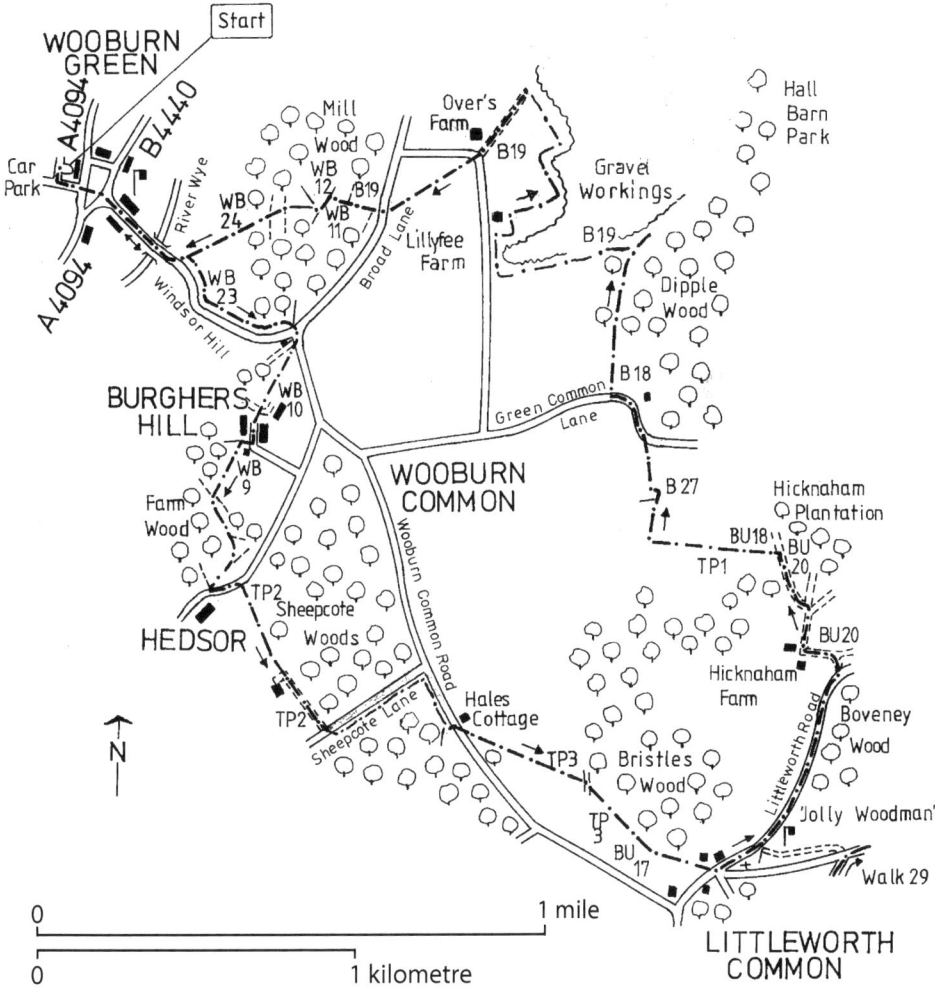

WOOBURN GREEN

Start

Car Park

Mill Wood

Over's Farm

Hall Barn Park

WB 12
WB 11
WB 24

B19

Gravel Workings

B19

River Wye

Broad Lane

Lillyfee Farm

B19

Dipple Wood

Windsor Hill

WB 23

B18

BURGHERS HILL

WB 10

Green Common Lane

WOOBURN COMMON

WB 9

B27

Hicknaham Plantation

Farm Wood

BU18
TP1

BU 20

TP2
Sheepcote Woods

Wooburn Common Road

HEDSOR

BU20

TP2

Sheepcote Lane

Hales Cottage

Hicknaham Farm

Boveney Wood

N

TP3

Bristles Wood

Littleworth Road

'Jolly Woodman'

TP 3

BU 17

Walk 29

0   1 mile

0   1 kilometre

LITTLEWORTH COMMON

127

WALK 28   Bourne End

Length of Walk: (A) 8.0 miles / 12.8 Km
                        (B) 5.7 miles / 9.1 Km
Starting Point: Car park by Bourne End Public Library.
Grid Ref: SU894875
Maps: OS Landranger Sheet 175
             OS Explorer Sheet 172 (or old Sheet 3)
             Chiltern Society FP Maps Nos. 1, 13 & 32
How to get there / Parking: Bourne End, 4 miles north of
     Maidenhead, may be reached from the town by taking the
     A4094 northwards. In Bourne End, fork left onto the A4155
     to the Shopping Parade, where a car park is signposted to the
     right.

Bourne End, although it has existed since at least the thirteenth century, has only developed from a hamlet into a small town in relatively modern times. Situated near the confluence of the River Thames and the Wye, which flows through High Wycombe, Bourne End's principal attraction is the River Thames and it is one of the most popular locations for sailing on the river.

Both walks follow the Thames Path along the beautiful stretch of river between Bourne End and the Marlow Bypass against the magnificent backdrop of Winter Hill. The routes then cross the river and climb through Quarry Wood to the ridge of Winter Hill, where panoramic views of the Thames Valley can be obtained, before dropping down into Cock Marsh, from which Walk B returns direct to Bourne End, while Walk A continues to the picturesque village of Cookham before making its way back to Bourne End.

Both walks start from the car park by Bourne End Public Library and take Wakeman Road out to the Shopping Parade. Here cross the A4155 and take Wharf Lane opposite, bearing right and following it to a road junction with a small traffic island with a tree on it. Still on Wharf Lane, bear slightly left here to reach a railway level-crossing. Now go straight on over the level-crossing into a boatyard where you bear right and take path WB45 to reach the Thames Path. Turn right onto this (path WB5, later LM1) and follow it along the riverbank for nearly half a mile until you leave the built-up area near a railway level-crossing at Spade Oak

Wharf, site of a former ferry. Here take the Thames Path (path LM2) straight on through a kissing-gate and continue to follow the riverbank for two miles (later on path MA1c), passing the end of **Walk 20** at the beginning of the second field.

Eventually Marlow Bypass Bridge is reached. Here turn right along the near side of the bridge to reach and climb a flight of steps to the A404. At the top, turn right then immediately left and take a fenced path crossing the river with views to your right of the picturesque riverside town of Marlow. Now continue along the grass verge to cross a bridge over Quarry Wood Road, then turn left, stepping over a crash-barrier and descending a flight of steps to this road. Turn right along the road and follow it until it crosses a bridge over a stream into Quarry Wood. At a road junction here, leave the road and take path B3 straight on through the wood, soon bearing left and climbing gently up a terraced path across the face of the hill. Near the top, the path bears right and climbs more steeply, eventually going up steps to a road. Do **not** join the road, but bear left onto path B4, another terraced path behind the roadside crash-barrier, following the contours of the hill through the wood. In places, extensive views open out through the trees in the winter months across Marlow and the Thames Valley to the hills above High Wycombe. Ignore a branching path to the right and after a third of a mile, join a drive. After another 20 yards, turn left onto a path through a belt of trees into a hilltop car park at Winter Hill with panoramic views of the Thames Valley.

Here cross a low bank to the left of the car park to take the upper of two paths along the hilltop. Now follow it until scrub forces you to join the road. At a road junction, go straight on, then just past a large red-brick house with security gates, turn left onto path C57. Follow this track downhill, ignoring lesser branching tracks, to reach Cock Marsh. Here turn left towards a gate and kissing-gate, but do **not** go through these gates. Instead turn right and follow a fence and hawthorn hedge along the edge of the marsh, a National Trust property. Where the hedge and fence turn left, **Walk A** bears half right across the marsh to a bridge under the Bourne End railway near two double-pole electricity pylons. Now omit the next paragraph.

Walk B goes straight on across the marsh to a gate and stile right of an electricity pole right of the last in a row of bungalows. Here go under a railway bridge, then turn left to reach the bank of the Thames. Now turn left onto the Thames Path (path C60), passing through a kissing-gate and under a railway bridge, then turn left up a flight of steps to cross a footbridge over the Thames on the side of the railway bridge. At the far end of the bridge, descend some steps, go through a gate and leaving the Thames Path, turn right onto fenced path WB5. On reaching the end of a gravel lane, bear left and follow it, ignoring a branching path to your right, to reach the A4155. Turn left onto this, passing Bourne End's Victorian church and the railway station to reach a mini-roundabout. Here turn right then immediately left onto fenced bridleway WB25 right of Lloyds Bank's car park to reach your starting point.

Walk A now goes under the bridge, passing through a large kissing-gate, then bears left for a few yards to avoid a drainage channel. As soon as possible, bear right across the marsh to join the Thames Path (path C60). Turn right onto this and follow it for over three-quarters of a mile to Cookham. On passing a boatyard, the path becomes macadamed and passes a riverside green. At the far end of this, turn right onto path C51 through a gate into the churchyard, passing the twelfth-century church with its fifteenth-century tower to the left and continuing out through gates to the busy but narrow A4094. The village centre is to your right and is well worth a visit. Otherwise turn left and take the A4094 over Cookham Bridge, built in 1867 to replace an earlier wooden structure, but now no longer suited to the amount of traffic it bears.

After passing a boatyard to the right, turn right over a stile onto path WB1. Now bear half left across a field with a fine view of Tower Hill with its eighteenth-century folly, Hedsor Tower, ahead to rejoin the riverbank near a bend in one of the four streams into which the Thames temporarily divides below Cookham Bridge. Now take path HD1a, following the riverbank until a fence blocks your way ahead, then turn left and follow it, later a hedge to a footbridge. Do **not** cross this, but instead turn sharp left onto path HD1, crossing the field to the corner of a hedge. Here keep straight on, following a right-hand hedge, swinging left then right around a small compound (now on path WB2) to reach a stile by a gate in the corner of the field leading to the A4094. Do **not** cross this stile, but turn right onto fenced path WB3, crossing the next field with views to your right of Hedsor Tower and the tiny hillside Hedsor Church further to your right, to reach a small gate onto Hedsor Road. Cross this and keep straight on along the concrete drive to Hollands Farm. At the farm, fork right through a gate and follow a left-hand fence, then the back of a barn. Now bear slightly left to a kissing-gate in a corner of the field. Here follow a left-hand hedge to further gates, then take path WB4, following a left-hand hedge, then an industrial estate fence, soon joining a raised concrete path alongside it. Where the fence ends, join Millboard Road and take it straight on over a bridge over the River Wye to the A4094. Turn left onto this road and where it forks, take the A4155 straight on. Just before the Lloyds bank on your right and a mini-roundabout, turn right onto bridleway WB25 back to your point of departure.

MARLOW

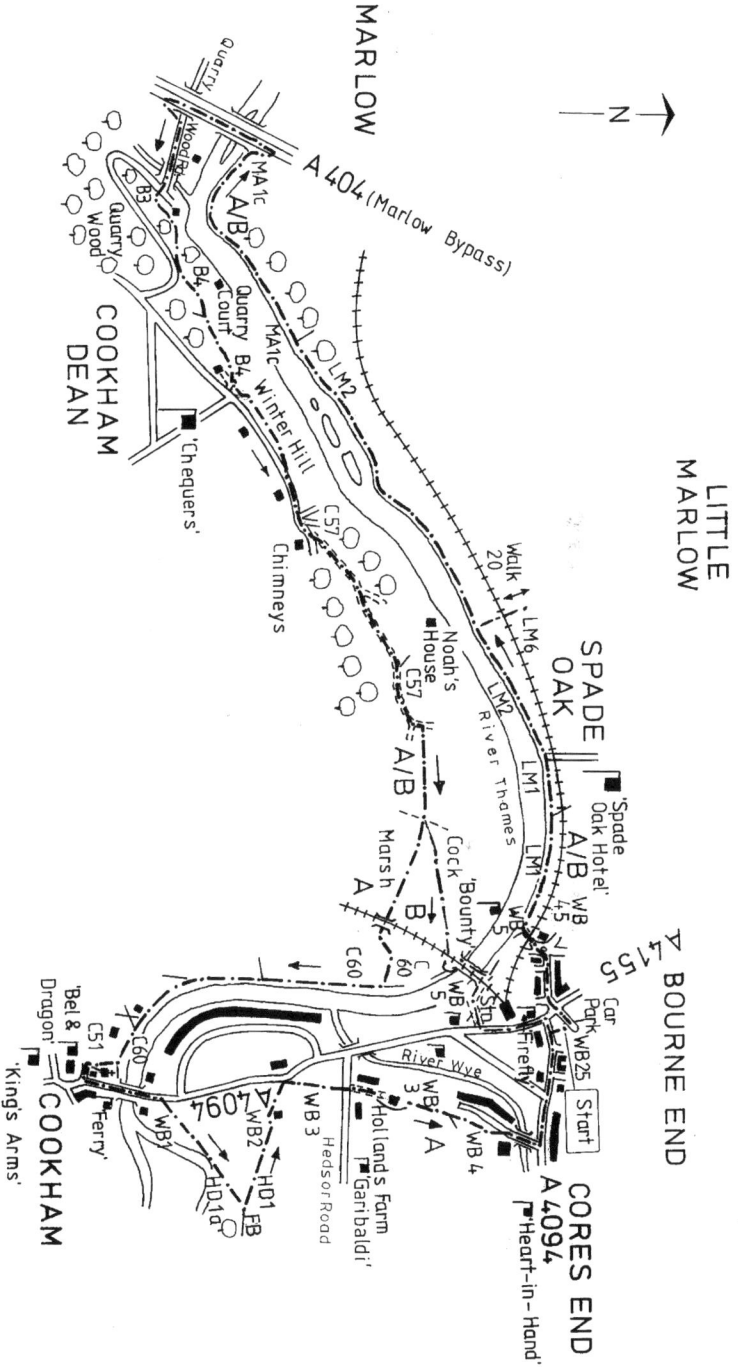

LITTLE MARLOW

N →

A 404 (Marlow Bypass)

Quarry

Wood Rd

MA1c

A/B

B3

Quarry Wood

B4

Quarry Court

MA1c

Winter Hill

COOKHAM DEAN

'Chequers'

Chimneys

C57

C57

A/B

Noah's House

Walk 20

LM2

LM6

LM2

LM1

LM1

River Thames

SPADE OAK

'Spade Oak Hotel'

A/B

WB

WB

5

Marsh

A

B

Cock

'Bounty'

C60

C 60

WB

5

Car Park

WB25

'Firefly'

BOURNE END

A4155

Start

CORES END

A4094

'Heart-in-Hand'

River Wye

Holland's Farm

'Garibaldi'

WB1

A

WB4

WB 3

Hedsor Road

WB3

WB2

A4094

HD1

HD1a

FB

'Ferry'

COOKHAM

'King's Arms'

C51

C60

'Bel & Dragon'

0   1 kilometre

0   1 mile

WALK 29   Burnham Beeches

Length of Walk: 7.4 miles / 11.9 Km
Starting Point: Green gates near café on Lord Mayor's Drive, Burnham Beeches.
Grid Ref: SU954850
Maps: OS Landranger Sheet 175
OS Explorer Sheet 172 (or old Sheet 3)
Chiltern Society FP Map No.24
How to get there / Parking: The main parking area of Burnham Beeches, 3.1 miles south of Beaconsfield, may be reached from the town or Junction 2 of the M40 by taking the A355 southwards for over 3 miles to reach Farnham Common. Just before the start of the shopping parade, turn right onto a road signposted to Burnham Beeches. At a crossroads at the edge of the Beeches, go straight on along Lord Mayor's Drive and park about 300 yards along it.
Notes: Paths in this area tend to be boggy even in dry weather.

Burnham Beeches, which serve as a ´green lung` and wooded playground for London, its western suburbs and the nearby dormitory towns and villages, represent a milestone in British conservation history. Their purchase in 1878 by the Corporation of the City of London, together with the acquisition of Epping Forest, shows public authority in Victorian England becoming aware of the need to conserve the countryside and take active steps to fulfil this requirement. Burnham Beeches also have a unique characteristic which is of interest to the countryman as well as the urban dweller: the gnarled ancient beeches which, in some cases, may be up to a thousand years old. They have survived this long because, until about 1820, they were regularly pollarded for firewood and for making charcoal. It is this treatment which has caused their fantastic shapes. The end result is that the Beeches resemble a primæval forest and contrast sharply with modern managed woodlands.

This walk is one of a particularly wooded nature, traversing the Beeches to Littleworth Common before passing through more woodland to cross the A355 near Collum Green. The next section, visiting the picturesque rural village of Hedgerley, is more open, before you return through more woods to Farnham Common and Burnham Beeches.

Starting from the green gates near the café at the western end of the Lord Mayor's Drive parking area, keep straight on along the drive for a few yards, then take the first forking road to the right, soon joining another road. Just past another gate at a left-hand bend, where Halse Drive is signposted, leave the road and take a path straight on into the woods, soon bearing right and starting to descend. Just before the path drops steeply to reach a stream, turn left onto a crossing path and follow it downhill and up again until you reach a five-way path junction. Here turn right onto a wide, gently climbing path and follow it straight on for some 300 yards to a road junction. Now take Mc.Auliffe Drive straight on for nearly half a mile, looking out for an ancient earthwork known as Hartley Court Moat to your right, part of the outer mound of which crosses the road. This earthwork is believed to be the site of a mediæval fortified homestead and farm. Just past this earthwork, at a road junction, turn right onto a bollarded macadam path to cross Park Lane at the edge of the Beeches.

Here take path BU9 straight on through a kissing-gate into Dorney Wood, following the obvious path straight on through the wood for a quarter mile, ignoring a branching permissive path to your right and eventually leaving the wood through a kissing-gate. Now take a fenced path straight on between fields to a kissing-gate by a corner of Twelve Acre Wood and take the fenced path straight on along the edge of the wood to a gate into a green lane leading to gates onto Common Lane by the 'Blackwood Arms` at Littleworth Common.

Turn right onto this road and at a T-junction by Boveney Wood Farm, turn right into Boveney Wood Lane. At a further road junction, take this lane straight on, then, at a sharp right-hand bend, leave it and take path BU23, a wide green lane, straight on. On reaching a gate and kissing-gate, follow a left-hand hedge straight on to a gate and stile into Staplefurze Wood. In the wood, follow its edge for nearly a quarter mile ignoring branching paths to the right. Where the path eventually leaves the edge of the wood, keep right at a fork and take path BU24 straight on through the woods for nearly half a mile, ignoring branching tracks to your right, to reach a stile and gates. Cross the stile and keep straight on to reach a gate and gap into Harehatch Lane. Turn right onto this road and follow it to the A355 near Collum Green.

Cross this busy road carefully and take bridleway HE1, a macadam private road, straight on to Pennlands Farm, once centre of the local brickmaking industry. Here take bridleway HE2, a fenced track, straight on, later becoming a hedged lane and reaching a road junction. Now take Kiln Lane straight on for a third of a mile to a T-junction in Hedgerley.

Turn left here into Village Lane, then, by the village noticeboard, **joining Walk 26**, turn right onto path HE13, a gravelly lane between the manor house and the attractive village pond. Take this lane straight on with views through the trees to your left of Hedgerley Church (see Walk 26) to reach a gate and kissing-gate at the far end of the lane. Go through the kissing-gate and **leaving Walk 26**, bear half right onto path HE11 across a field to a stile into Hanging Wood just right of the far corner of the field. Now take an obvious path straight on uphill through the wood. On leaving the wood, take a fenced path between fields straight on to reach another wood, then turn left over a footbridge into a corner of the wood, soon leaving it again through a fence gap. Now go straight on across the field to a gate and stile near a tall Scots pine on the edge of a wood ahead.

Cross the stile and turn left onto Collum Green Road. At a road junction, bear half right onto path SP37 into Stoke Wood. Now follow the waymarked path, keeping left at the first fork and right at the second. On reaching the fence of an underground reservoir, turn left and follow it, immediately bearing right and eventually reaching the entrance to the reservoir. Cross this entrance, then turn right onto a fenced path, skirting the reservoir and then passing between gardens to reach a private road. Turn right onto this road and follow it for about 100 yards. Just past a house called 'Footprints', turn right into a narrow path between garden fences (still SP37) and follow it to Templewood Lane on the outskirts of Stoke Poges.

Turn right onto this road and after some 300 yards, at a right-hand bend, turn left between bollards onto wide bridleway SP44, following the edge of Brockhurst Wood with views to your left towards Stoke Poges. After nearly half a mile, follow the bridleway turning right then left but still on the edge of the wood. On reaching a junction of tracks, bear half right onto path SP28, the drive to Hornbeam Cottage. Where the drive turns left through a gate, leave it and go straight on over a stile by a gate and take an obvious path straight on through beechwoods. After some 350 yards, cross a culvert and take fenced path FR16 straight on through the woods, later between gardens, to reach Parsonage Lane at Farnham Common.

Turn right onto this road, then, at a bend, turn left into Victoria Road to reach the A355. Cross this road and take a macadam path straight on, soon joining Kingsway. At road junctions, turn left into Green Lane, then right into Hawthorn Lane. At the edge of Burnham Beeches, turn right again into Bedford Drive and after about 90 yards, turn left onto a well-defined path through the trees which soon emerges into open grassland. Here bear half left, following a worn path along the edge of the grassland area, eventually keeping right at a fork to reach Lord Mayor's Drive near your point of departure.

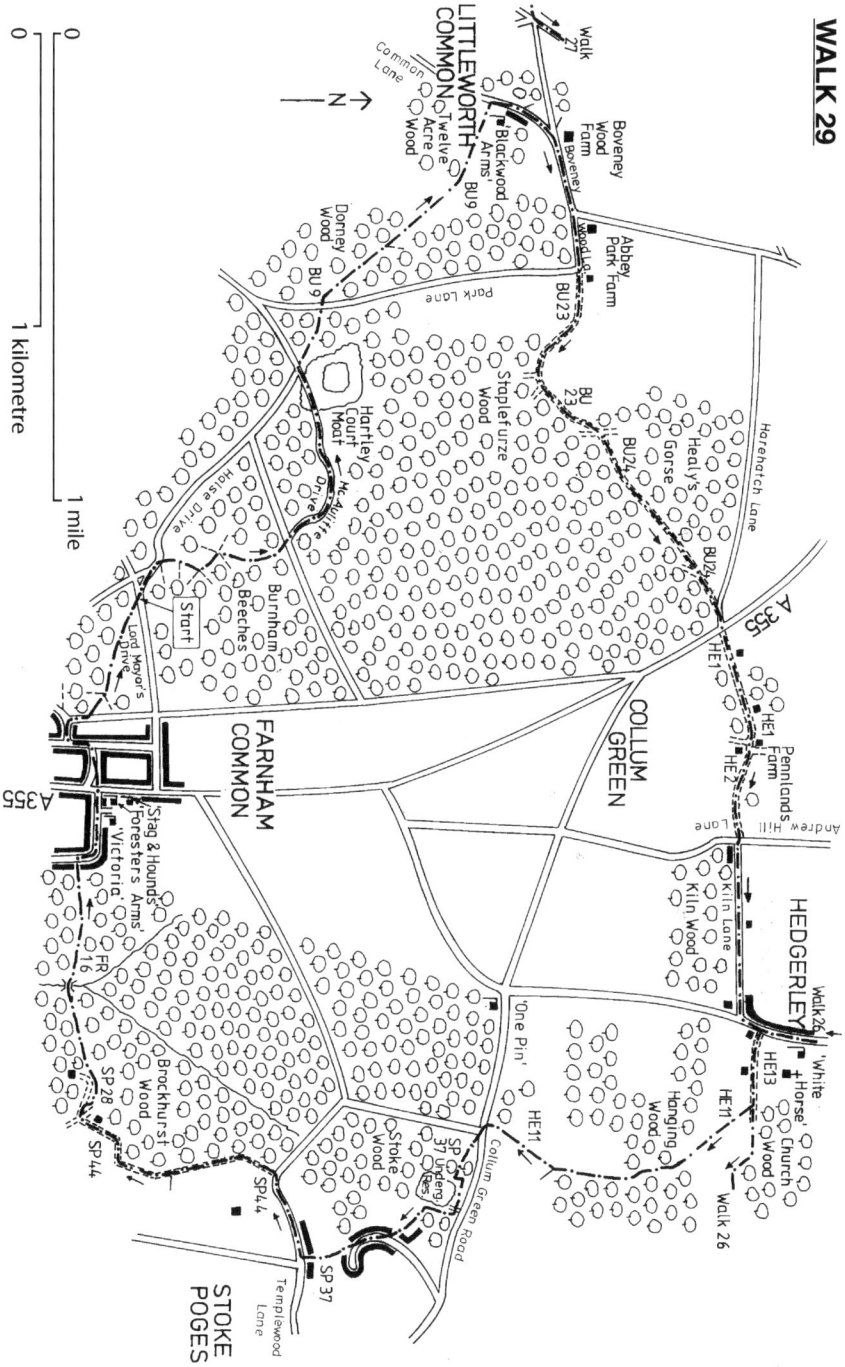

WALK 29

LITTLEWORTH COMMON

Boveney Wood Farm

Walk 27

Common Lane

Twelve Acre Wood

Blackwood Arms

Boveney

Abbey Park Farm

Dorney Wood

BU 9

Park Lane

BU 23

Healy's Gorse

BU 23

BU24

BU24

Horehatch Lane

Staplefurze Wood

Hartley Court Moat

Halse Drive

HE Little Drive

Beeches

Burnham Beeches

Start

Lord Mayor's Drive

FARNHAM COMMON

COLLUM GREEN

A355

HE1

HE1

HE1

HE2

Pennlands Farm

Andrew Hill Lane

Stag & Hounds

'Foresters' Arms'

'Victoria'

A355

FR 16

Kiln Lane

Kiln Wood

HEDGERLEY

Walk 26

White Horse

Church

HE13

HE11

Wood

Hanging Wood

Walk 26

Brockhurst Wood

SP 28

SP44

'One Pin'

Collum Green Road

Stoke Wood

SP 37 Underg'd Res.

HE11

SP44

SP 37

Templewood Lane

STOKE POGES

0 _____ 1 kilometre

0 _____ 1 mile

N →

135

WALK 30   Stoke Poges

Length of Walk: 9.9 miles / 16.0 Km
Starting Point: Junction of B416 (Gerrards Cross Road) &
                Pennylets Green at Stoke Poges.
Grid Ref: SU982844
Maps: OS Landranger Sheet 176
            OS Explorer Sheet 172
            (part only) Chiltern Society FP Maps Nos. 22 & 24
How to get there / Parking: Stoke Poges, 3 miles southwest of
   Gerrards Cross, may be reached from the junction of the
   A40 and B416 at Gerrards Cross Common by taking the
   B416 towards Slough for 2.8 miles. On reaching the village,
   turn right into Pennylets Green and look for a suitable on-
   street parking space.
Notes: Several parts of the walk tend to be swampy even in dry
   weather.

Stoke Poges, the name of which derives from the thirteenth-century marriage of the heiress of the manor, Amice de Stoke, to her guardian's son, Sir Robert Pugeys, has gone into history as the setting of Thomas Gray's 'Elegy written in a Country Churchyard'. However, the churchyard where the poem is believed to have been written lies in fields preserved by the National Trust more than a mile from the modern village centre which bears little resemblance to the rural idyll which Gray depicts.

The walk soon leaves this enclave of suburbia behind and crosses the wooded Stoke Common, which was preserved for the village in 1810 after a lengthy battle to prevent its enclosure. You then pass through the picturesque village of Fulmer and turn southwards to explore Black Park with its attractive lake and fine coniferous woods and Langley Park with some rare trees and its Georgian mansion, before returning across country to Stoke Poges.

Starting from the junction of the B416 (Gerrards Cross Road) and Pennylets Green, take the B416 northwards for over a quarter mile. Just past its junction with Vine Road, turn right through gates, then fork right onto part of bridleway SP35, following a right-hand fence and earth bank marking the boundary of Stoke Common. Follow this earth bank for three-quarters of a mile, turning sharp left after a quarter mile and later right. After the earth bank bears right again, ignore a path merging from your left, then, at a crossways by a Beeches Way marker post, leaving the earth bank, take a path straight on across the common, disregarding all branching and crossing tracks. Eventually you emerge through a bridlegate onto Stoke Common Road opposite Top Lodge. Turn right onto this road and left at a road junction onto Windmill Road to enter the village of Fulmer, the name of which is a contraction of the mediæval 'Fouwelemere' meaning 'lake of birds'.

Despite its proximity to London, Fulmer, unlike most of its neighbours, has been allowed to survive largely unaltered with its attractive seventeenth-century church, eighteenth-century pub and two interesting manor houses nearby. The church, unusual for the Chilterns in being constructed of brick, was built by Sir Marmaduke Dayrell in 1610 and contains a monument to him.

Pass the 'Black Horse' and the church, then, by a telephone box, go through a kissing-gate by the gates to Church Farm onto path FU2. Now follow the farm drive straight on and where it turns right, leave it and take a fenced path straight on beside the concealed Alder Bourne, eventually passing through a copse to a kissing-gate. Here bear slightly left across a field to cross a stile by a gate right of an electricity pole, then bear slightly right to a kissing-gate and footbridge just right of a corner of the field. Now go straight on across the next field, walking parallel to a hedge to your right to reach a kissing-gate into a clump of rhododendrons, then continue along a fenced path, eventually joining a macadam drive at the edge of Home Wood. At a T-junction, take a path straight on through rhododendrons to reach another drive. Turn right onto this and where it forks, bear left and follow it straight on for 300 yards to a kissing-gate beside electronic gates onto Fulmer Common Road.

Turn left onto this road and follow it straight on for over a quarter mile, ignoring the branching Black Park Road and Cherry Tree Lane. About 100 yards past Cherry Tree Lane, opposite a house called Amber Wood, turn right through a gap by a gate into the publicly-owned Black Park and take fenced bridleway WX23, bearing slightly right. At a three-way fork, turn right, soon veering left. Ignore a branching path to your right and a branching track to the left and at a T-junction, turn right, disregarding two branching paths to the left. Now at a crossways, turn left, leaving the bridleway and following a wide stony track signposted 'Car Park / Lake' and known as Queen's Drive for half a mile. At a clearing at the far end of this drive, take a macadam path straight on, bearing slightly right then turning left to reach Black Park Lake.

Turn right here and follow its shore to the far end of the lake. Now take path WX4 round the end of the lake and continue past the Lakeside

Café. Just past the café turn right onto a gravel track, soon bearing half left and taking a track straight on through the woods for half a mile, disregarding all crossing tracks, until you reach the A412 dual-carriageway virtually opposite Billet Lane.

Cross this busy road carefully and take Billet Lane straight on for a quarter mile. Just before the first right-hand bend, just past the entrance to Highfield House on the left, turn right through a fence gap into Langley Park. Inside the park, bear left across an open grass area to the right-hand corner of a car park. Now take a path behind the car park parallel to Billet Lane and follow it for a third of a mile along an avenue of wellingtonias until you reach a gap by a gate leading to a track. Here turn left, then, by a black gate, turn right onto path WX10 following a concrete wall at first, soon with an orchard to your left and Langley Park to your right. On reaching metal gates into the corner of a walled garden, bear slightly right and follow the garden wall. By the far end of this wall, turn right through a kissing-gate onto fenced path WX12 and follow it straight on for a third of a mile with views of Langley Park House to your right, built in the eighteenth century by the second Duke of Marlborough as a residence closer to London than Blenheim Palace.

Having crossed a footbridge and passed through a kissing-gate, the path becomes unfenced to your right and continues along the edge of George Green Field. At the far side of the field, go through another kissing-gate and take a green lane straight on to a road junction at George Green, which was formerly known as Westmoor Green.

Here go straight on, wiggling slightly right into George Green Road. Take this road through the village to the A412, then turn left along the main road to reach a footbridge near the 'George`. Cross the footbridge and retrace your steps on the other side of the road to a kissing-gate just before the traffic lights. Turn left through this and a second kissing-gate onto path WX7, crossing a field to cross a stile. Now turn left and follow a grassy track to the far end of a long narrow field. Here the track turns right and becomes fenced, soon bearing left then right. At one point you pass through two gates before the track turns right again and later left. On reaching the hedge of Deadman's Lane, you then turn right again and walk parallel to the road until you join it. Turn sharp left onto this road. After 70 yards, turn right onto path WX6, climbing steps and bearing half left through a belt of trees to a stile. Cross this and bear half left across a field, passing just right of a clump of pine trees to reach the far corner of the field. Here go through a gap in a thick hedge passing a redundant stile to reach Gallions Lane. Cross the lane and a stile by a gate opposite onto path WX3, following this green lane, then a concrete road past Bell Farm with its sixteenth-century farmhouse and Wexham Park Hospital to reach Wexham Road near Stoke Green.

Cross this road and turn left along its footway for about 100 yards,

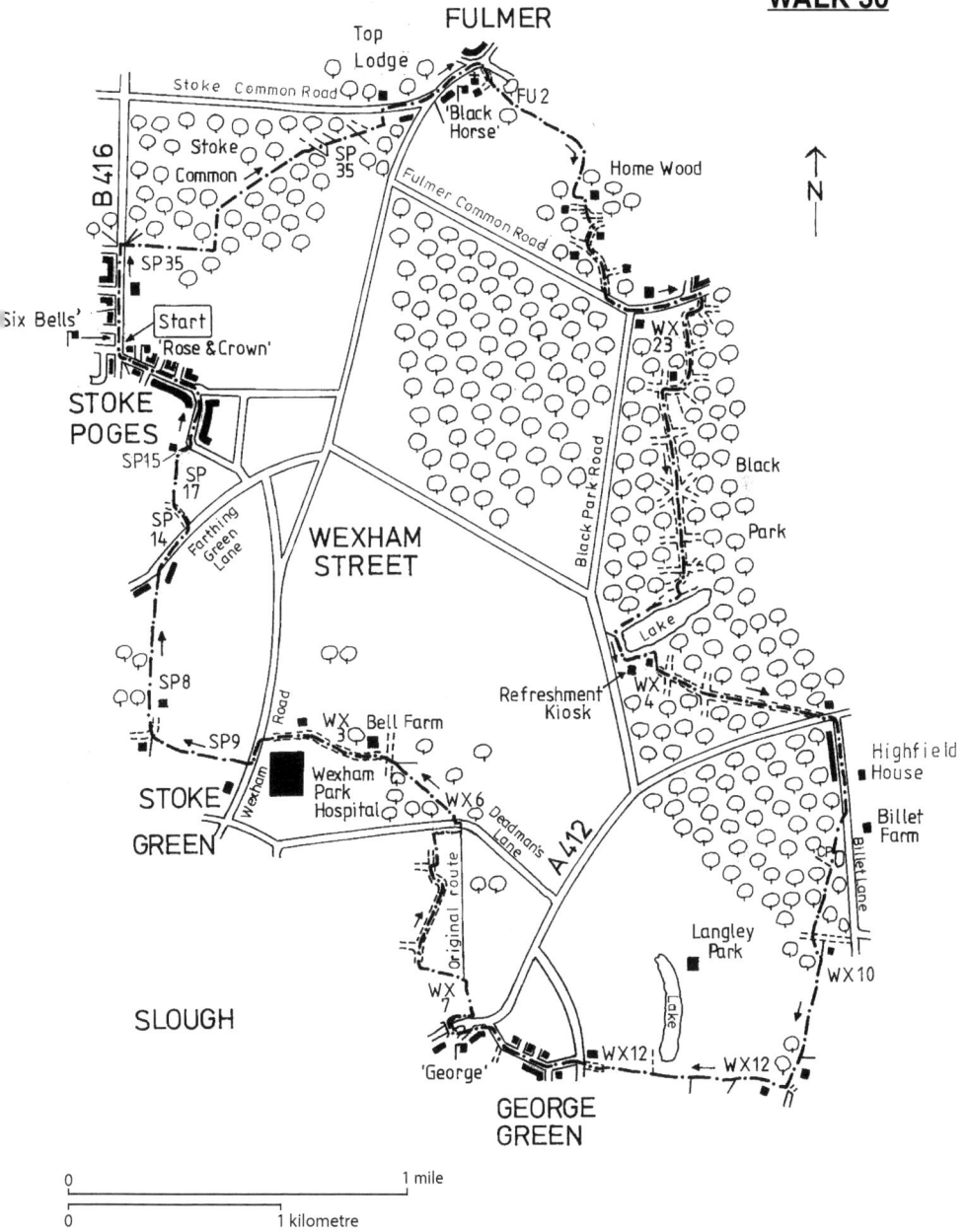

WALK 30

FULMER

Top Lodge

Stoke Common Road

'Black Horse'

FU 2

Stoke Common

SP 35

Fulmer Common Road

Home Wood

N

B 416

SP 35

'Six Bells'

Start

'Rose & Crown'

WX 23

STOKE POGES

SP 15

SP 17

SP 14

Farthing Green Lane

WEXHAM STREET

Black Park Road

Black Park

Lake

SP 8

Refreshment Kiosk

WX 4

SP 9

WX 3

Bell Farm

Wexham Road

Wexham Park Hospital

WX 6

Deadman's Lane

Highfield House

Billet Farm

STOKE GREEN

A 412

Original route

Langley Park

Lake

Billet Lane

WX 10

SLOUGH

WX 7

'George'

WX 12

WX 12

GEORGE GREEN

| 0 | | 1 mile |
| 0 | | 1 kilometre |

139

then turn right over two stiles onto path SP9. Go straight through a car park and across a field to a kissing-gate under an oak tree, then follow a left-hand hedge straight on to cross a footbridge and stile. Here bear half right across a field to a gate and stile in the top corner of the field leading onto a drive. Cross the drive and a stile opposite onto path SP8, following a right-hand hedge to cross a further stile. Now take a fenced path straight on to a gap by a disused kissing-gate, then continue beside a left-hand hedge to two more kissing-gates. Go through these and follow a left-hand fence straight on to cross a stile at the far side of the field, then follow a fenced path to a macadam drive. Take this drive straight on to Farthing Green Lane, then turn right onto this road and follow it for some 200 yards. Now turn left through a kissing-gate onto path SP14, following a stony track ahead into a green lane. After about 130 yards, just before the far end of the green lane, turn right through a kissing-gate onto path SP17 and bear slightly left across a field to a kissing-gate, then keep straight on to a small gate in a wooden fence by a red-brick building. Here turn right onto fenced path SP15 to a kissing-gate leading to a bend in School Lane at Stoke Poges. Take this road straight on to a T-junction, then turn left into a road called Hollybush Hill, passing the 'Rose and Crown' to reach your point of departure.